Birdwatching
in Kent

Birdwatching in Kent

by
Don Taylor

Meresborough Books
1985

Published by Meresborough Books, 7 Station Road,
Rainham, Gillingham, Kent. ME8 7RS

ISBN 0905270932

Printed by Mackay of Chatham Ltd, Chatham, Kent.

Contents

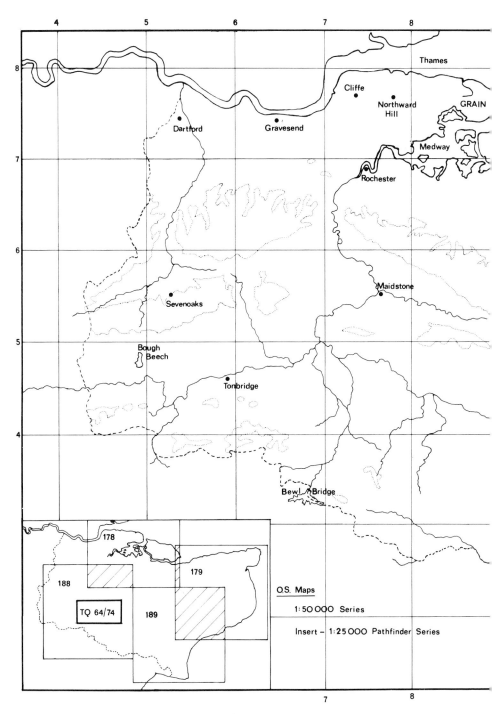

Thames

4   5   6   7   8

Cliffe

Northward
Hill

GRAIN

Dartford

Gravesend

Medway

Rochester

Sevenoaks

Maidstone

Bough
Beech

Tonbridge

Bewl Bridge

178

179

188

189

TQ 64/74

O.S. Maps

1:50 000 Series

Insert – 1:25 000 Pathfinder Series

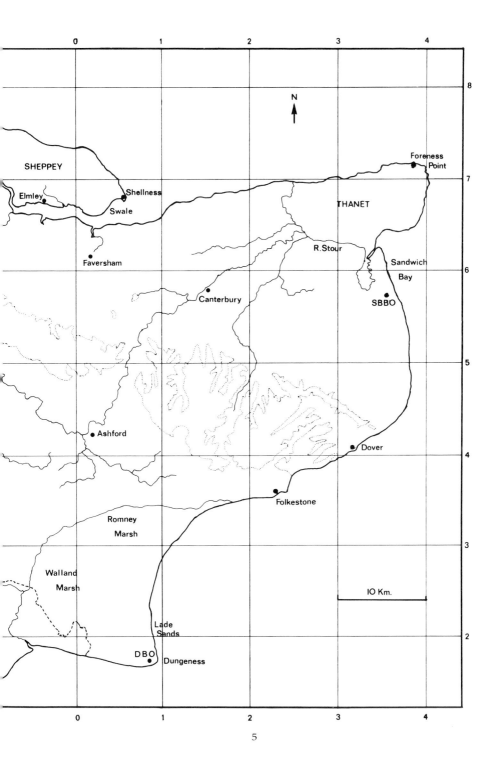

Red-necked Phalarope (above) at Cliffe Pools in August 1983.

Grey Phalarope (below) at Lade Pits in March 1983.

Foreword

The county of Kent is widely regarded as one of Britain's most productive birdwatching regions. It owes this reputation largely to its geographical situation on the main landbird migration routes to and from the Continent, and to its position dominating the seabird migration 'funnel' of the southern North Sea and the English Channel. On the coast and inland, too, is a highly varied landscape of different habitats which are attractive to a wealth of migrant and resident species.

There is certainly no one better qualified than Don Taylor to write about its birds. For twelve years he was editor of the Kent Ornithological Society's annual *Kent Bird Report*, and he co-edited the latest county avifauna *The Birds of Kent*, published in 1981, with a second edition in 1984.

In this present book he has filled a long-standing need for a quick-reference guide to the 'where and when' of all Kent's birds. The Systematic List section of the book will be an invaluable at-a-glance reference which will prove especially useful to anyone taking up birdwatching for the first time, and to birdwatching visitors to the county. He describes a number of very different birdwatching trips for each month of the year, giving details about tides, wind direction and access points.

Other sections in this book, however, make it much more than a guide to the birds in just one county. Initial chapters contain much useful advice and information for any newcomer to birdwatching, and I hope they will be read far outside the confines of Kent. Don Taylor rightly describes birdwatching as a hobby which can be taken up at many different levels of involvement, from garden-bird watching to an all-consuming fanaticism. He describes his own experiences of the 'purely for fun' side of the hobby – day and year species-listing – and his more 'scientific' studies of the birds on his own 'home patch'. Both facets of an interest in birds can be rewarding in their own different ways, and the well-written accounts give a fascinating insight into how one expert birdwatcher approaches his hobby, and the pleasures and frustrations which he derives from it.

Best of all, this book will stimulate a greater knowledge and experience of Kent's birds among a wider public. In my view, there is no better way to strengthen public appreciation – and hence the preservation – of Kent's already over-pressured countryside and the wildlife which it contains.

Peter Grant

Introduction

This book is concerned primarily with showing ways of enjoying birdwatching in Kent. The inspiration came from my own enjoyment and considerable involvement, through the Kent Ornithological Society, with the birds of this county, and my desire to share that pleasure with others.

Birdwatching is becoming an increasingly popular pastime and I am convinced that one of the reasons for this is that you can select a level of interest to suit your own particular life style. For some, this may simply mean an appreciation of garden birds, or occasional days out – you should find some useful suggestions for these. Others find particular satisfaction from studying one small area regularly – I describe my experience of a local area study that gave me a great deal of pleasure. Visits to Bird Observatories give others an opportunity to study bird migration, or to assist with bird ringing. Some like to concentrate on watching seabird movements and they are happy to sit for hours, in all weather conditions, gazing out to sea. Others like the challenge of listing – building annual, county, or life lists of species satisfactorily identified. I describe a single day during which I saw more than 130 species, and a year when I managed to see 210 species in Kent; following which I make suggestions for regular birdwatching trips during a calendar year. For a dedicated few there is the possibility of developing a life-long professional interest.

A concern for the welfare of our birds may lead to an interest in the conservation of habitat and membership of the *Kent Trust for Nature Conservation*. Again, there are different levels at which you can become involved or offer your services.

The *Kent Ornithological Society*, which was founded in 1951 to study and record all aspects of the avifauna of Kent, plays a major part in conservation by providing the facts – the numbers and distribution of birds throughout the county. Anyone interested in contributing records, or getting involved with surveys and census work, will find much scope for this by joining this Society. In return, there will be the opportunity to share the interest with others, while receiving regular information about the county's birds in the form of Bulletins, Newsletters and Annual Reports. *The Birds of Kent*, published by the Kent Ornithological Society in 1981 – with a second edition in 1984 available from Meresborough Books – is an essential reference for serious birdwatchers living in the county.

The *Royal Society for the Protection of Birds* has various local groups operating in the county that meet regularly, and among other activities raise money for the purchase of hides on reserves. In Kent there are already four RSPB Reserves, at Dungeness, Northward Hill, Church Wood and Elmley.

With its strategically sited geographical relationship to the Continent, its lengthy coastline and wide variety of natural and man-made habitats, Kent attracts a considerable number of birds – I describe the major habitat types and mention some of the associated bird species.

Recording the numbers of different species over periods of time, or for different areas, as I have already suggested, is one of the challenges that many birdwatchers readily accept. By the end of 1983 the total number of species on the Kent list had risen to 356, of which 328 have been seen since 1970 – these are all included in the Systematic List.

It is interesting to note the influence of the increased interest in birdwatching on the Kent species-list. There are other factors, of course, notably the establishment of the two Observatories, at Dungeness and Sandwich Bay, and the natural expansion of species' ranges, like the Collared Dove, Savi's and Cetti's Warblers, which have colonised Britain in recent years. During 1900–49 just 23 species were added to the county list, while 59 more have been added since. This trend seems likely to continue and 1984 already looks like equalling, if not surpassing, the 1976 record of five new species in one year. I can think of three North American gull species – Ring-billed, Franklin's and Bonaparte's – which are surely due to occur soon, judging by the number of records elsewhere in Britain – a challenge for gull enthusiasts.

The ability to identify birds correctly is one of the pleasures that, to me, is essential for the enjoyment of birdwatching. It is a skill which produces new challenges all the time. In its most sophisticated form, it is an exacting art, but again, it is possible to set your sights at a level to please yourself.

You will need a good pair of binoculars and a reliable field guide. There is such a varied choice of optical aids available that I would recommend seeking advice from experienced observers. Try out several different pairs of binoculars before committing yourself. As far as field guides are concerned, it is again difficult to know what to recommend, but one of the best recent books is undoubtedly *The Shell Guide to the Birds of Britain and Ireland* by James Ferguson-Lees, Ian Willis and J.T.R. Sharrock (Michael Joseph). There is nothing like experience in the field, however, and watching with someone with that experience can save many hours of error and frustration. Join the KOS or local RSPB members' group and go on their field meetings.

Try to get to know the common species in all stages of plumage, and learn their various calls and songs. The ear is an invaluable aid, not only in identification, but also in locating birds. Get into the habit of using a notebook in the field, do not rely on your memory. Try to record precisely what you see, as you see it. Simple, outline sketches can help to show the distribution of plumage colour, but it is more useful to know the different feather groups, so that you can relate the colours to them. So much can be of value when trying to identify a bird. Not just colour, but size, shape, behaviour, manner of feeding or flight, etc. As your knowledge increases, you will begin to learn what characteristics separate one species from another. I have made some personal comments to this effect in the Systematic List.

Finally, I take the opportunity to thank all those who have given me encouragement and support for this project. In particular the Kent Ornithological Society, who gave me permission to use their records, and Bob Bland, whose frequent visits to Langley Park Farm provided much of the data for the chapter on local area studies. I am also greatly indebted to Tricia Pringle, Peter and June Stoodley, and Peter Grant for their helpful criticisms of the original draft.

Don Taylor

Franklin's Gull

Kent Habitats

This county is blessed with a very diverse range of habitats, both natural and man-made. Here and in the systematic list section I mention a number of specific localities where you are most likely to find particular species, but I also recommend that you explore other areas of similar habitat, where possible. Of course, the uniqueness of natural sites like Dungeness and managed Reserves like Elmley have no parallels, but one of the pleasures that I derive from birdwatching is the opportunity that it provides to visit areas relatively undisturbed by other humans. On the other hand, sharing a hide on a Reserve provides you with an opportunity to gain from the experience of others. Learning to identify birds at sea can be difficult, too, without guidance. As with all things, a degree of compromise is required.

The large scale 1:50,000 Ordnance Survey maps are invaluable for discovering new areas and locating footpaths, while the even larger, 1:25,000 Pathfinder Series maps are quite excellent.

In the following paragraphs I list a number of habitat types and mention particular localities and species commonly associated with them.

Chalk Downland

The North Downs, stretching the length of the county, from Shoreham in the west to Dover in the east, provide a rich and varied habitat for quite a number of species. Some open grassland remains, but much of the escarpment, which is too steep to plough, is now covered with thorn, yew, ash and beech woodland. The combination of grassland and mature trees attracts the Green Woodpecker, while the open scrub is much favoured by the Linnet and Yellowhammer. Of particular interest are the outcrops of mature beeches, under which good crops of beech mast, in the winter months, will invariably attract a few Bramblings with the Chaffinches. Hawfinches, too, find the beech and ash to their liking and a few pairs breed regularly in these areas. Most members of the tit family can be expected, including the Coal Tit amongst the yews and the Marsh Tit in the deciduous woodland copses. A few pairs of Long-eared Owls probably breed regularly, but nocturnal visits are needed to establish their presence, by hearing the adults calling, unless you are fortunate enough to stumble across the distinctive, mournful calls of the young in mid-summer. Regular observation will undoubtedly produce several raptor species. In addition to Kestrel and Sparrowhawk, Buzzard and possibly Hen Harrier and even Merlin, in the winter, might also be expected.

Woodland and Parkland

The variety of woodland habitat in the county provides a great range of species with suitable sites for nesting, feeding and roosting. Some of the primary woodlands that remain still attract breeding Grey Herons, as they have done at Chilham, for example, for hundreds of years, while the heronry at Northward Hill, which now holds over 200 pairs, is the largest in Britain. Rookeries are very widespread and can be found in all sorts of woodland, while the commonest breeding species are likely to be Chaffinch, Wren, Robin and Willow Warbler.

Some species have more specialised requirements. The Redstart prefers mixed woodland and parkland, with old timber to provide nest holes, while the Wood Warbler, which has declined as a breeding species, favours sessile oak, mixed with birch and bracken. The Nightingale breeds quite commonly, with higher concentrations in the woods around Canterbury, but it requires dense undergrowth to provide sufficient cover for nesting. Sweet chestnut coppice and young conifer plantations provide suitable breeding habitat for Tree Pipits, Woodcock and a few pairs of Nightjars, but this last species too has declined in recent years, as has the Grasshopper Warbler, which also likes young conifer plantations and dense, low undergrowth. However, Golden Orioles have recently started to breed regularly in a number of woodlands, mainly in east Kent.

The dense conifer plantations attract Goldcrests and Coal Tits, while a few pairs of Crossbills may stay to breed, following the occasional irruption. The Firecrest too has recently colonised this habitat, favouring the mature Norway spruce. The Pinetum at Bedgebury is renowned for attracting finches to roost, including the Hawfinch, Brambling and Siskin.

A few pairs of Hobbys and Sparrowhawks do breed, but the latter species, sadly, is still persecuted by some gamekeepers and one wonders whether this persecution prevents some of the larger raptors from breeding successfully, when much of our woodland seems so suitable.

Few woodland walks are complete without hearing, or seeing, a Great Spotted Woodpecker, or watching a Nuthatch pecking at an acorn which it has wedged in a cleft, or almost running over the bark as it hunts insects.

One important aspect linked with the parkland and public open spaces in this county, is the presence of small lakes, often created by damming streams. As Kent has few natural lakes, these man-made waters provide an important habitat for waterfowl. Large flocks of Canada Geese frequent Mote Park and the Leeds Castle grounds, often flighting between the two. During the breeding season, many disperse to small ponds scattered over the farmland to nest and raise their broods. Moorhens, Coots, Little and Great Crested Grebes are usually present too, along with Mallard and Tufted Duck, the numbers of which increase during the winter months. Visits from less common wildfowl, such as Wigeon, Gadwall, Pochard and Goldeneye can occur during cold spells. The muddy fringes may attract migrant waders during the spring and autumn, and in the more boggy, reed-fringed areas Water Rail, Snipe and even Jack Snipe may be found.

The typical short grassland and mature tree habitat that occurs in some of the older parks is much favoured by the Green Woodpecker, often to be seen on the grass, pecking for ants. Both the Great Spotted and Lesser Spotted Woodpecker may also be seen, while the thin, high-pitched song of the Treecreeper and the piping call of the Nuthatch are frequently heard. The deer-grazed pasture and ancient oaks of Knole Park still attract the Redstart to nest.

Treecreeper – a typical species of mature parkland.

Wealden Farmland and Hedgerows

On the pasture and arable meadows of the Weald, the Lapwing is a common sight throughout the year, but the large flocks are more often seen in the autumn and winter months, unless the ground becomes snow-covered and they disperse to milder climes. The Golden Plover, too, favours certain meadows, particularly those below the greensand ridge between Sutton Valence and Boughton Monchelsea. Here, flocks of up to 500 can be seen, most often in March. Black-headed Gulls are the most common gull species to follow the plough, while both Grey and Red-legged Partridges are·to be expected. Flocks of hungry Rooks frequently blacken the green fields while they search for leatherjackets.

Hedgerows provide invaluable cover for many birds. Thrushes, warblers and finches of various species find the variety of bushes and trees to their liking, for nesting and feeding. The more mature hedges, with occasional trees, attract such species as Lesser Whitethroat, while those with broad bases provide cover for the Grey Partridge and Yellowhammer to nest. As you walk along hedgerows during the winter months you are likely to disturb such species as Long-tailed Tits, Bullfinches and Magpies, while away from the Weald the Corn Bunting's distinctive jingle can frequently be heard. Little Owls are fairly widespread and may be seen perched or hunting along the hedgerows.

Rivers and Wetlands

The many tributaries of the Darent, Medway and Stour attract such resident species as Grey Wagtail and Kingfisher, while the alders, which are often associated with damp areas, are much favoured by Siskins in the winter months.

The excavation of gravel along the Medway Valley below Aylesford has increased the attraction of this area, not only for wintering wildfowl, but also for common breeding species such as Meadow Pipit and Yellow Wagtail. However, the Stour Valley, again as a result of man's intervention, now provides richly diverse breeding sites for a great variety of species. Extensive reedbeds are scarce in Kent and those at Westbere and Stodmarsh are renowned for the attractive and successful Bearded Tit, the rare Savi's Warbler and the now resident Cetti's Warbler, which has recently colonised Britain, breeding first in the Stour Valley. Sadly, the Bittern does not breed regularly, but the drumming of Snipe and the song of the Water Rail are attractive features of the spring, while large numbers of migrant Reed and Sedge Warblers, and their attendant Cuckoos, breed commonly. Its proximity to the coast, too, helps to make it an obvious site for rarer vagrants such as the Purple Heron and Spotted Crake. In the winter months, the number and variety of waterfowl increases, while one of the main attractions can be the Hen Harriers, as they gather towards dusk to roost in the reedbed at Stodmarsh.

Wetlands generally are on the decline and much of Romney and Walland Marsh is now well drained. However, the numbers of Bewick's Swans wintering there are as high as they have ever been. It is not unusual to see a flock of over 100 grazing on the winter wheat, or on what pasture remains. Mute Swans, too, form quite large flocks. Similar habitat exists on the Wantsum Marsh, north of the Stour Valley, and on the North Kent Marshes.

Reservoirs

As there are so few natural, open, inland waters, the development of two large reservoirs in the west of the county has provided a most attractive new habitat, particularly as certain areas have been set aside as Nature Reserves. While Bewl Bridge, which straddles the border with Sussex, has footpaths around much of its perimeter, providing quite good viewing of the many inlets, Bough Beech has its public vantage points concentrated along the road across the north end. From there you can expect to see most of the visiting waterfowl and many other regular and rarer visitors. The list of species recorded there alone is well over 200 now.

Both reservoirs have provided breeding sites for Great Crested and Little Grebes, Mute Swans and Canada Geese, and several duck species. At Bough Beech, one of the most fascinating sights in the summer months is the breeding of the Little Ringed Plovers, whose best interests are being considered when the nests are covered with wire cages, to prevent predators such as Carrion Crows from taking the eggs.

Both reservoirs have also provided supporting evidence for the overland migration of waterfowl and waders. Brief visits by such species as Common Scoter, Bar-tailed Godwit and Common Tern in spring, often coincide with the main up-Channel passage off Dungeness, while in autumn quite a variety of waders and terns drop in for short visits. The Black-necked Grebe, too, is fairly regular.

Ospreys occur annually, on migration through the county, and more often than not some of the records concern individuals visiting one or other of these fine reservoirs.

The influx of waterfowl in the winter months is one of the major attractions. The Black-throated Diver is almost an annual visitor to Bewl Bridge, while the rarer grebes, such as Red-necked and Slavonian, can also be expected. Large numbers of Wigeon are attracted to the grassy meadows sloping down to the water's edge at Bewl Bridge, while both reservoirs can expect a few Goosander and Smew during cold spells.

Gravel Pits

Many gravel workings, particularly those that have become Reserves, now provide invaluable refuges for many species, not just waterfowl. Some, in co-operation with the owners, have been worked with the interests of the birds in mind. Those at Sevenoaks and Dungeness are prime examples. Without gravel workings there is little doubt that the Little Ringed Plover would still be a scarce migrant, rather than a regular breeding species. Other new breeding species, attracted in particular to the gravel pits of the Dungeness Reserve, include Mediterranean Gull and both Sandwich and Roseate Terns. The Common Gull, a rare breeding species in southern England, also nests there successfully.

In addition to the breeding species like Great Crested Grebe, Mute Swan, Tufted Duck and Coot, the gravel pits attract many wintering wildfowl, like Goldeneye and occasionally Goosander, while migrant waders, such as Common and Green Sandpipers are frequent visitors. Regular watching will inevitably produce rarer species from time to time.

Without man's interest in excavating sand, relatively few Sand Martins would be nesting in Kent. Not surprisingly, the breeding distribution of this species coincides closely with the geological map showing the distribution of greensand in the county.

Green Sandpiper – a frequent visitor to gravel pits and other wetland habitats.

Coastline and Estuaries

The long and varied coastline is a veritable haven for many birds. Facing north, east and south, migrants from all three directions can be expected, according to the season and prevailing weather.

Dungeness, the unique shingle spit that juts out into the English Channel, provides an ideal point from which to observe seabird passage in spring and autumn, while southerly winds in summer may bring Manx Shearwaters within sight of the shore.

While concern will continually be expressed about the effect Nuclear Power Stations will have on the environment, the effect for certain birds so far has been positive. The Black Redstart is attracted by these man-made cliffs and a large percentage of the county's small breeding population is associated with them, or similar industrial buildings. The warm water outflows too provide an attraction, close to the shore, for feeding gulls and terns. Locally known as the 'patch', the Dungeness outflow offers an ideal opportunity to study these species, with the possibility of a rarer one turning up, or a skua creating havoc amongst them.

The warden at the Bird Observatory will invariably be in the area and will welcome anyone interested in the activities of this strategically sited ringing station. He will be happy to direct you over the trapping area and tell you what is about. By becoming a 'Friend of Dungeness' you will not only help to finance the work of the Observatory, but also receive regular information about the birds there. It can be most exciting when there has been a fall of migrants. Amongst the large numbers of commoner species, one always hopes to find something more unusual. In the autumn, such species as Pied Flycatcher and Redstart, and the rarer Wryneck and Icterine Warbler, are quite regular.

Burrowe's Pit – on the RSPB Reserve close to the Nuclear Power Station, has attracted new breeding species.

The gravel pits in the area also attract numerous species. In addition to those pits on the Reserve, including the ARC pit and New Diggings either side of the road, there are others on Dengemarsh and a little further north at Lade. If you prefer, it is easy to get away from the 'popular' spots and visit the other pits and the coastline towards the Brooks in relative peace and quiet, while the numerous patches of scrub and gorse may well produce their own interesting passerine migrants.

Working north, towards Greatstone, Lade Sands attracts large numbers of feeding gulls and waders when the tide is out, and is an area much favoured by the Sanderling. All along this coast, in the winter months, flocks of Great Crested Grebes form, while divers can sometimes be seen close to the shore. Folkestone Harbour and Copt Point are also good areas to study gulls, the latter in particular regularly attracts Mediterranean Gulls. Shags, too, may be seen here, usually in the winter months.

Folkestone Warren provides a sheltered haven for passerine migrants, while in winter the foreshore attracts Purple Sandpipers and Rock Pipits. The chalk cliffs from here northwards now attract breeding Fulmars and Kittiwakes, while the successful Herring Gull has spread onto the rooftops in Dover itself. Stonechats and Black Redstarts are both specialities of the area, the former breeding on the clifftop gorse and the latter, either on the old wartime buildings on the cliff or around the town.

The sheltered, wooded valley near the lighthouse at St. Margaret's Bay is proving to be an excellent site for observing migrant passerines. Regular observation here has produced a fascinating range of common and rare visitors.

North of Deal there is Sandwich Bay, the site of Kent's second Bird Observatory. Here too, visitors are welcome and membership will help to keep you informed about the birds of this particular region. The trapping area produces a wide variety of passerine migrants, including such eastern rarities as Yellow-browed and Pallas's Warblers at regular intervals. It is quite a long walk to the point and back, but it can be most rewarding. In winter, a large flock of Snow Buntings is invariably present and occasionally a few Shore Larks can be seen. At high tide, roosting waders can be observed well from close to the point, while offshore it is not unusual to see Eider.

Stonar Lake occasionally attracts rare grebes and duck in the winter, while Pegwell Bay, at the mouth of the Stour, is another good area for waders. As the tide rises, a good selection can often be seen well from the shore just south of the hoverport.

The geographical position of Thanet makes it an obvious landfall for Scandinavian migrants in the autumn. Despite being heavily built up, all the small wooded plots, the open areas along the coast from North Foreland to Foreness Point, the golf course and Northdown Park, will attract a good variety of migrants. It is also an excellent site for seawatching, while the rocky shoreline and sheltered bays attract Turnstone and a wintering flock of Purple Sandpipers.

Westwards, between Minnis Bay and Reculver, there is an open stretch of undeveloped coastline, with the Wantsum Marsh to the south, which, with regular observation, has also produced a fascinating range of species. The shingle here attracts Little Terns in summer, Snow Buntings and possibly Shore Larks in the winter, while offshore in autumn, seabird movements can also be observed.

Beyond Whitstable lies one of the most important areas in the county for waders and wildfowl – the North Kent Marshes, the combined area formed by the estuaries and surrounding marshland of the Swale,

Medway and Thames. During the winter months, the mudflats in the river estuaries attract thousands of waders, but at each high tide they need to rest at undisturbed roosts, providing a good opportunity to see them well and to estimate their numbers. The roost sites vary a little according to the tides, but in the Swale the shingle beach at Shellness, the saltings at Harty and the Elmley Reserve are all used regularly. Large flocks of waders such as Oystercatchers, Grey Plover, Dunlin, Knot and Bar-tailed Godwits can be seen. In the Medway, two of the important roosts are on private pools within Kingsnorth Power Station and the Grain Refinery, which are favoured by Spotted Redshanks and Greenshanks in the autumn. Fields adjacent to the estuary are often used on the south Medway, while in the Thames the shingle at Yantlet Creek and the pools at Cliffe provide sanctuary for more waders. Large numbers of Ringed Plovers frequently roost at the latter site.

Oystercatchers – flying to roost in the Swale.

The estuaries of the Swale and Medway also play host to Brent Geese and Red-breasted Mergansers, among other waterfowl. The Medway Estuary is of international importance for wintering wildfowl, regularly holding between ten and twenty thousand duck, including over one per cent of the northwest European totals of Teal, Wigeon, Pintail and Shelduck. At the mouth of the Medway, the outflow from the Grain

Power Station also attracts large numbers of terns and gulls in the autumn, where they can be seen extremely well at close range.

In the summer months, the coastal margins of north Kent attract breeding species such as Shelduck, Oystercatcher, Redshank and Ringed Plover, with colonies of Black-headed Gulls and Common Terns on isolated tracts of saltmarsh.

Large flocks of White-fronted Geese winter regularly on Sheppey and at Cooling, while several birds of prey find the marshes equally attractive. Small numbers of Hen Harriers, Short-eared Owls and Merlins have always been regular visitors, while the now regular occurrence of the Peregrine on Sheppey is a most exciting recent development. One of the most impressive birdwatching experiences this county can offer must be the sight of thousands of ducks and waders wheeling over Elmley as a Peregrine streaks in, intent on a meal.

Langley Park Farm – the reed-fringed lake which attracts a good variety of species.

A Local Study: The Birds of Langley Park Farm

For many birdwatchers the study of one small area holds an irresistible attraction. Some may find sufficient interest in an area of one particular habitat, or in studying an individual species, but for me it is the variety that holds an absorbing fascination. The more diverse the habitat, the greater the variety of species you can expect to record. In that respect one local patch, which became rather special to me, provided considerable interest.

Between 1970–81 I studied the bird life of Langley Park Farm, near Maidstone. It is some 120 hectares and consisted then of orchard, hops and arable farmland, with a few uncultivated patches. A small stream that runs through the farm was dammed in the early part of this century creating an attractive lake, surrounded now by reeds and fairly mature trees. Its presence is the principal reason why the surprisingly high total of 150 species was recorded in the twelve years. Of these, 82 occurred in every year, while a total of 60 species bred, 31 in every year. On average about 110 species could be expected annually, depending on the number and frequency of visits made.

To get to know your own study area really well, you need to visit it as frequently as possible. This should be borne in mind when selecting a site. I actually found this one by studying an Ordnance Survey map that roughly covered the area between my home and place of work. Seeing a lake marked, I made a point of visiting it. I suppose I was spoiled from the start. On virtually my first visit there, in January 1970, I not only saw a good variety of common species, but also flushed a Jack Snipe and saw both Bearded Tit and Great Grey Shrike. Having gained the owner's permission to watch over the whole area, I visited the farm on average twice a week for the next twelve years.

From April 1974, Bob Bland joined me. Working shifts and living closer, he was able to make even more frequent visits, so that the farm received excellent coverage, being visited on average about 220 days each year.

Another important aspect of studying an area is not only visiting it at different times of the year, but also at different times of the day. Early morning is often a particularly fruitful time, when newly arrived migrants are most active and when the majority of species are most vocal. But visits at dusk are equally important to learn about roosting behaviour, while a few nocturnal visits may be necessary to record such species as Tawny Owl. This, strangely enough, was the one common species that failed to occur, to our knowledge, during the study period – a little surprising when the other four owl species were recorded. I feel sure, however, that had either of us actually lived on the farm, we would have heard one calling.

Species that are common elsewhere can often be quite rare locally and they acquire a different status on your own patch. The different seasons, marked by the arrival and departure of migrant species, offer a continuously changing pattern. With the grubbing of orchards in favour of arable land, one also gets an insight into the natural balance and an opportunity to assess man's influence. Sometimes the changes can be linked with similar patterns elsewhere in the county, but on occasions they may result purely from alterations on the farm. The grubbing of about 600 metres of mature hedgerows was undoubtedly the greatest loss during the period of the study. Hedgerows, being the motorways of the natural world, are an essential element in our landscape and, when allowed to mature, provide nest sites for a number of species that help control the insect pests that feed on the cereal crops.

Sadly, this farm was sold in 1982 and the new owner soon grubbed the mature and young orchards alike, pulled down the hop wires and poles, and ploughed up as much land as was possible. It began to look like a prairie farm. Maybe I should have continued to record the changes, but somehow my interest and enthusiasm deserted me.

Perhaps the best way to show the pleasure that I gained from studying this local area is to describe the annual pattern of events. The fact that this invariably changes from year to year is probably one of the reasons why I was able to maintain my interest for so long.

An analysis of the records shows that the following totals of species were recorded for each month:

J	F	M	A	M	J	J	A	S	O	N	D
88	89	91	106	106	85	91	108	103	102	90	88

Not surprisingly, the greatest variety occurs during the migration periods, but it is interesting to note just how many were recorded during the winter months, particularly as the lake is very small and often freezes over. Species totals in excess of 60 were frequently recorded for each month, with peaks of 85 in April 1975 and October 1976. As far as daily visits are concerned, it was not too unusual to record 40 to 50 species.

January – February

The winters have generally been relatively mild, with just occasional, short, cold spells. However, in 1979 Kent experienced the severest winter conditions since 1962/63 and the summary for that period makes fascinating reading (*Kent Bird Report No. 28*).

The extreme conditions produced 72 different species on the farm, the highest January total throughout the twelve years. Unlike most New Year's Days during the study, the farm was snow covered, with deep drifts on 1st January 1979. It was most picturesque. The lake was completely frozen over, remaining so until late February. The visit on that day was most remarkable for the number of species seen. The total of 51 included a good variety of waders, with a single Golden Plover, two Jack Snipe, 32 Snipe, four Woodcock and a Green Sandpiper. To see Kingfisher, Grey Wagtail and Hawfinch on the same day was also quite unusual, while typical cold weather movements involved 300 Lapwings flying southwest and 400 Woodpigeons to the north.

The movement of Lapwings according to the weather conditions was just one interesting aspect of this local study. Often they would disperse at the onset of snow, but on occasions I can well remember seeing flocks huddled in the white blanket, presumably aware that it was going to thaw quickly. In milder conditions 800 flew northeast in late January 1981. Numbers actually on the farm varied from none, when it was snow covered, to about 400, during mild spells.

When the lake is open, a few Mallard, Teal and Tufted Duck can be expected, while Wigeon and Shoveler are scarce visitors. Mute Swans too are surprisingly rare, three in January 1975 being the first to be seen on the lake, with an immature present throughout January 1978 and a pair in January 1979, which were usually on the open water just downstream of the farm. During the 1979 cold spell, Goosanders were seen flying over on three occasions and up to 17 Teal were present. This last species was far commoner in the early seventies, with a peak count of 85 in January 1970, but the numbers and frequency of sightings, for no apparent reason, declined steadily during the twelve years.

Birds of prey are relatively scarce, apart from Kestrels, and Sparrow-hawks were seen on only four dates during January–February, being more frequent in March and again in the autumn. However, a Hen Harrier turned up during the January 1979 cold spell and a second flew north in January 1981. There are only two records of Short-eared Owls and one of these also occurred in January 1979, while up to five

Long-eared Owls were present in January 1978. One or two pairs of Little Owls are usually resident and, when not located by the sound of agitated tits and Chaffinches, you can expect to hear them calling at dawn or dusk.

The attractive Water Rail is essentially a winter visitor and up to five can usually be expected. During cold spells, with snow on the ground, they are much more easily seen. The changing status of the Coot makes another interesting story. In the early years over 20 would be present in the winter months, but their numbers too declined and following a disastrous breeding season in 1976, when a mink was seen eating the eggs at one nest and only one young was raised, only one or two pairs have returned. When the lake becomes completely frozen over, any remaining Coot quickly disappear. In 1979 none was seen until the thaw came in late February.

Several wader species are regular visitors during the winter months. A few Golden Plover may join the Lapwings, or fly over from time to time. Snipe numbers have fluctuated considerably, with a maximum of 50 in January 1976, while one to three Jack Snipe can be expected each winter, with an unexpected total of six on 8th January 1977. One or two Woodcock may regularly be disturbed from the thick undergrowth during the winter, but up to five were present in January 1979. The Green Sandpiper has become more regular as a winter visitor, with singles favouring the food and shelter to be found along the stream. Quite unexpectedly, two Ruff stayed for a few days during a cold spell in late January and early February 1976, while four Dunlin flew west in February 1979 – the only records of both species.

Woodpigeon numbers are much influenced by the availability of food and, being a gregarious species, they can wreak havoc on rape and cereal crops. In the late seventies, rape was sown in the winter and this attracted over 1,000 Woodpigeons in late December 1977 and early January 1978, but flocks of 100–200 are more usual. While Great Spotted Woodpeckers are resident, the Green is relatively scarce in the winter months, but the Lesser Spotted can be expected occasionally. One of the first rarities to be seen in the study area was a Woodlark. Three were present in a hop garden on 27th January 1970 – this remains the only record. The presence or absence of Skylarks is again influenced by the severity of the weather. Flocks of 50–100 are fairly regular, but up to 400 were present in late January 1979. The status of Meadow Pipit has also fluctuated, being virtually absent during most winters, though there were three years when small flocks of 20–30 were present, often feeding in the hop gardens. The Grey Wagtail is an occasional winter visitor to the farm and it breeds further down the Loose valley.

The winter thrushes provide another source of interest, their numbers too being much influenced by the availability of food. The Redwing is generally quite scarce during January–February, but the numbers of Fieldfares fluctuate considerably. While a good crop of apples remain in the orchards, flocks of up to 1,000 may occasionally be seen, though much smaller flocks are more usual. However, in 1979 the numbers increased to about 4,000 by late January, but then dwindled rapidly as the food source became depleted.

During the first four winters, from one to four Bearded Tits could be found feeding in the willow-herb along the stream, or in the reeds surrounding the lake, but since then they have become scarce passage migrants. The Marsh Tit too has become quite a rarity, occasionally visiting the farm in early autumn, but all the other tit species and the Treecreeper can be expected during the winter months, with flocks of up to 40 Blue Tits searching for food on occasions. A single Nuthatch was seen in February 1980, only the third record for the farm.

A Great Grey Shrike has occasionally wintered and one memorable moment occurred in January 1977, while I was watching a Short-eared Owl. The owl had alighted in barley stubble when a shrike suddenly appeared and hovered over it, swooped and hovered again. It repeated this several times before flying off to alight on the top-most branch of a pear tree.

Of the crow family the Magpie has been relatively scarce, with no summer records at all – its status at Langley is that of a winter visitor and passage migrant! Pairs of Jays and Carrion Crows are resident, while Jackdaws and Rooks occasionally gather in quite large flocks, usually feeding in the stubble or on winter cereal crops, before flying off to roost. A quite spectacular movement occurred on 9th January 1977, when over 1,000 circled up into dark clouds, as a cold front moved through. They then flew off northeast, towards their roost, followed by a further flock of 100 Jackdaws.

The numbers and variety of finches present during January–February are again determined by the availability of the seeds on which they feed. Up to 300 Tree Sparrows sometimes remain through the winter, but a count of 500 in January 1980 was exceptional. Counts of 100–200 Chaffinches were recorded in just five winters, but Bramblings have always been relatively scarce during the winter months. Only a score or so Greenfinches are usually present, though there were 100–150 in January 1970 and 1974. The wintering population of Goldfinches frequently numbers less than 10, though a flock of 50 was present in 1973 and 1976. Linnets invariably disperse in the autumn and in some winters no more than five may be seen, but in three others there were flocks of 100–150 for part of the time. One of these flocks arrived in mid-February 1974 and amongst the Linnets I discovered an attractive male Twite, which even sang occasionally. This species is exceptionally rare away from the coast in Kent and it made me wonder whether the Linnets too had been wintering on the coast, before flying inland.

The relatively scarce Siskin and the more common Redpoll often feed in alders and birches. We planted some alders along the stream in the early seventies and they are only now maturing sufficiently to attract these species, so their numbers have remained low during the winter months, the only exception being a flock of 50 Redpolls in February

1976. Small flocks of 10–12 Bullfinches are usually present. The only larger one, involving 30 birds, occurred in January 1972, when the ground was snow-covered. Hawfinches occur occasionally, but more often than not the record involves just singles flying over.

The Yellowhammer is another species that has changed its status from that of a winter visitor to an occasional breeder. Small flocks can be expected in the winter months, with a maximum of 100 in January 1971. The Reed Bunting's status on the farm was somewhat confusing early on. I assumed, in ignorance, that it was a resident. However, careful recording soon revealed that it was not unusual for none to be present in late summer, showing that the breeding population, which increased from three to sixteen pairs during the twelve years, was migratory. Numbers increased again during the autumn and in the winter months 40 or more were often present, feeding with the finches and roosting in the reedbed, with up to 70 in February 1977 and 1980. Corn Buntings too provided some interesting observations. Generally rather scarce visitors, they were discovered roosting at the lake in December 1976, with a peak count of 120 the following January. Smaller numbers continued to use the roost for the next two winters, but it was virtually abandoned thereafter.

April 9th, 1975 – an unexpected cold spell that suspended breeding for many species.

March–May

The weather during spring has a very marked influence on the pattern of bird life. Warm spells in March and April can encourage early breeding and the early arrival of summer visitors. Cold spells in April and May can delay migration and suspend breeding, while heavy rains and strong winds may have a devastating effect on breeding success. Examples of all these characteristics of spring became evident during the study.

Noting the dates on which song is first heard can provide interesting comparisons from year to year. Not all song is necessarily related to the establishment of breeding territories and one of the pleasures I enjoyed each spring was hearing the beautiful, fluty, descending phrases of four to five full-toned notes uttered by the migrant Redwings. Bramblings too have sung while on passage through the farm.

Early March may not see much change, but the willows are in bud and the blackthorn blossoms, and when the fields are ploughed, large flocks of Black-headed Gulls and small groups of Pied Wagtails – worth checking for the Continental White Wagtail – will be attracted to the easily accessible food. At this time up to 500 gulls can be expected, but only three or four Common Gulls are usually present for every 100 Black-headed Gulls. Very few of these two gull species are seen after early April, by which time most are at their breeding colonies on the coast. However, a northerly passage of the larger Lesser Black-backed Gulls can be expected, mainly during April, when there have been day totals of up to 30.

A warm spell produces a feeling that spring is arriving, but it is often short-lived. I well remember 9th March 1977 when exceptionally warm weather encouraged toads to mate, several butterflies to fly and a Chiffchaff to appear. However, the latter was probably an overwintering bird rather than a genuine early migrant.

Mid-March can produce early migrants; three in particular invariably arrive in March and the earliest dates on which they have been recorded at the farm are as follows:

Chiffchaff   12th   Wheatear   13th   Sand Martin   14th

On the lake, the Tufted Duck members normally increase to a peak of about 20 at this time, while Coots often begin to nest. In the hop gardens the flocks of Tree Sparrow occasionally increase to around 400, with up to 300 Chaffinches and 30 Bramblings. The returning winter thrushes often form quite large flocks, with up to 100 Redwings and an exceptional count of nearly 1,000 Fieldfares in 1981. A thin, but steady, northerly movement of Meadow Pipits and, less perceptibly, an easterly movement of Chaffinches provides more evidence of the changing seasons, as March occasionally storms into April.

Two other migrants that occur less regularly at this time are Black Redstart and Firecrest. The arrival dates of the latter are quite fascinating. In four springs males were first seen on 29th March, twice on 1st April and once on the 5th. Since the Bearded Tit ceased to winter, there have been three spring records of one to four birds, all between 1st–15th April. Another species that quickly became very scarce was the

Grasshopper Warbler. In 1970 singles were present and in song between 1st–7th May and two autumn migrants were seen, but there have only been two records since. They used to breed regularly just north of the farm, until the Park Wood Industrial Estate was developed!

Another interesting aspect of spring migration is the up-Channel movement of seabirds and waders. "What has that to do with the farm?" you may ask, but on occasions certain birds take a more direct route overland. Probably only a few are witnessed, but two Kittiwakes flew northeast on 26th March 1981, three Whimbrel on 9th May 1981, with three singles in three different years, all on 23rd April, while seven Bar-tailed Godwits also flew northeast on 6th May 1980.

By mid-April, depending on the prevailing weather conditions, one can expect new summer visitors to arrive almost daily and a summary of the mean arrival dates recorded at the farm, with the earliest dates in brackets, follows:

Chiffchaff	24 March	(12/3)	Sedge Warbler	24 April	(5/4)
Willow Warbler	8 April	(3/4)	Whitethroat	26 April	(14/4)
Sand Martin	13 April	(14/3)	Turtle Dove	28 April	(10/4)
Blackcap	17 April	(3/4)	Lesser Whitethroat	2 May	(16/4)
Swallow	17 April	(6/4)	Garden Warbler	4 May	(27/4)
Cuckoo	17 April	(9/4)	Swift	8 May	(26/4)
House Martin	23 April	(15/4)	Spotted Flycatcher	11 May	(1/5)
Reed Warbler	23 April	(11/4)			

An analysis of all the arrival dates suggests that the spring of 1981 was particularly early, with five of the earliest dates being recorded during mid-April. Occasionally, one can be fortunate and actually witness an arrival of migrants, as on 29th April 1978, when from out of a low cloud appeared a flock of about 30 Swallows, followed by 12 Yellow Wagtails – an exceptional number for the farm – and then six Turtle Doves. More often an early-morning visit follows an overnight arrival of migrants. One such day was 26th April 1977. During the morning the following species were present: a cock Ring Ouzel, four Wheatears, the first two Yellow Wagtails, the first Redstart and Whinchat, the earliest Swift and eight Sand Martins. In the evening there was no sign of most of these species, but there were seven Wheatears and at least 25 Swallows.

Not only are summer visitors arriving, but winter visitors are departing and it is interesting to compare departure dates from year to year. The most regular winter visitors are the two thrushes and their mean departure dates, with the latest in brackets, are:

Redwing 16 April (30/4)   Fieldfare 2 May (14/5)

Others, such as Jack Snipe, Brambling and Siskin are not quite so regular at the farm, but out of interest their latest dates are:

Jack Snipe 1 April   Brambling 28 April   Siskin 11 May

One of the regular features of spring at Langley is the arrival of the Reed Warblers. It is often early May, or even mid-month before all the breeding pairs are back, but their repetitious, churring song is one of the characteristic sounds from the reeds surrounding the lake, where up to 13 pairs breed annually.

May, too, can be an exciting month, with a wide variety of interest. A few winter stragglers may remain, resident species will have fledged young and most of the summer visitors will be involved with breeding. While observing and recording all this, one also anticipates the possibility of rarer visitors. An Osprey circled low over the lake in May 1970, a Montagu's Harrier flew north in 1981 and Hobbys have been seen in May in four different years, with the earliest on 17th April 1980.

June–July

Reading through my descriptions of the weather for these months, I found an amazing range, from 'unseasonably cold and dull', through 'unsettled', 'periods of heavy rain and strong winds', to 'mainly dry and warm' and 'exceptionally hot and dry'. Such are the vagaries of our climate.

Much of June was usually spent watching and recording the success, or otherwise, of the breeding species, particularly the later migrants. But there are other interesting aspects to note. Lapwings often commence their post-breeding dispersal fairly early in the month and flocks can be seen flying over, mainly to the northwest. In the early seventies Teal and occasionally Shoveler were seen, associated with the mid-summer dispersal of various duck species within the county. By the end of the month a few Black-headed Gulls can be expected again and maybe a few Herring and Lesser Black-backed Gulls will fly over. Also, post-breeding flocks of Linnets and Greenfinches are gathering to feed on the seeding grasses.

Some of the most unexpected and exciting events have been recorded during June. A Woodchat Shrike, which arrived on 28th June 1977 and remained until 2nd July, is the rarest species to have occurred. A Raven, which is most unusual in Kent, was seen in June 1981, but probably the most extraordinary event was the arrival of a pair of Marsh Warblers in 1980. They set up territory and eventually raised two young successfully – the first conclusive evidence of this species breeding in the county for forty years!

The list of species that bred successfully, or attempted to breed, is long, but quite a number of them only bred occasionally, or maybe just once. I do not propose to list, or mention, them all, but simply to comment on some of the more interesting aspects. On the lake Little Grebes bred in just three years, while the Tufted Duck has not bred since 1974. Young Water Rails were only seen in one year, though there were occasional summer records in others. The Sedge Warbler is a relatively scarce spring migrant and breeding was only proved in one year.

Little Grebes – a successful breeding pair.

Elsewhere on the farm, a pair of Kestrels fledged three young on just one occasion, Lapwings bred successfully in four years, while a pair of Snipe fledged four young once, in June 1976. Cuckoos bred annually, with Reed Warblers acting as hosts most of the time, though Dunnocks did so occasionally. One pair of Long-eared Owls bred in 1975, but strong winds in June unfortunately shook the nest so much that two of the three young fell out and died. Great Spotted Woodpeckers bred regularly, but sadly, they were also responsible for pecking a hole into a Lesser Spotted Woodpecker's nest and taking the young, on one of the rare occasions when that species attempted to breed.

While mentioning Lesser Spotted Woodpecker, I am reminded of the one occasion when I witnessed the display flight of the female, in December 1975. It consisted of two delightful, rather moth-like flights, with the wings held high over its back, as it 'floated' from branch to branch. One of the fascinations of studying a local patch is getting to know its birds well, some of them as individuals, and learning more and more about their behaviour. I well remember a Great Tit that mimicked the call of a Redstart one autumn; it genuinely had me fooled for a day or two. Little incidents like these can give great pleasure, or cause frustration!

Back to the breeding species. Somewhat mysteriously, though one pair of House Martins bred successfully in 1970, there have been no subsequent attempts, even though birds were always present during the summer months. Willow Tits bred regularly and it is interesting to watch them excavating a hole in a dead, usually rotten, willow stump.

For some reason, Long-tailed Tits have rarely bred successfully on the farm. More often than not the nests that we found were robbed and deserted. The only successful pair I recall built their nest high in the dense foliage of a Scots Pine, but most of the others were low and more accessible. Why do they nest so early, when there is so little foliage in which to hide their nests?

Whitethroat – commenced breeding again in 1974 following the population crash five years earlier.

Whitethroats suffered a population crash in 1969, primarily as a result of drought in its winter range in the Sahel zone of Africa, and it was interesting to watch the slow recovery of numbers on the farm. None bred successfully until 1974, increasing to three pairs in 1977 and four in 1978–79. The number of breeding pairs of Willow Warblers fluctuated considerably, with up to eight in 1974–75, but only one in 1978. The Pied Wagtail has only bred once and the Yellow Wagtail has never bred on the farm, though an adult, feeding two fledged young in late June 1981, must have nested fairly close by.

During July one becomes aware that the long period of autumn passage is commencing. At Langley, the concentration of Whinchats in autumn has never ceased to amaze me. They may often be present from early July until mid-October, with the peak numbers, usually up to 10 and a maximum of 16, occurring in early September. Balanced on top of the barley, or perched on the fence posts or wire, they are relatively easy to count. Another regular autumn migrant, probably in similar numbers, is the Sedge Warbler, though they are not so easily seen. They too start appearing in mid-July, but have passed through by the end of September.

Other, more local, species start to disperse and both Kingfisher and Grey Wagtail often move up stream to the farm in July. Migrant waders can also be expected and a Green Sandpiper is often present along the stream, while there are several records of Whimbrel flying southwest during July.

Of the less common occurrences there have been a few worthy of note. Single Hobbys were seen in four years, three Crossbills flew over in 1974, a Cetti's Warbler arrived for a five-week stay in 1981, a flock of 1,000 Swifts flew high to the west in 1980, while a pair of Red-backed Shrikes was present in 1977.

August–October
Certain weather conditions during the autumn may be expected to produce particular species, or patterns of behaviour. Black, thundery clouds may be preceded by large flocks of House Martins, or Swifts. I well remember 19th October 1976, when about 400 House Martins flew east under a heavy rain cloud. But more often in these conditions, where insects are concentrated in the upcurrents, Swifts can be seen feeding, as in August 1971 when I saw at least 150 in one flock.

Of the eighteen species of waders on the farm list, thirteen have occurred during August. Coastal as well as freshwater species migrate overland, as in the spring. Three Oystercatchers flew southeast in 1980, while in 1978 a flock of about 40 Knot and 14 Bar-tailed Godwits flew low to the southwest. Another flock of 12 Bar-tailed Godwits flew west in 1981. Single Greenshanks have made their presence known on three different occasions by uttering their distinctive call as they flew south, while a Spotted Redshank flew southwest in August 1979. This last bird caused considerable confusion at the time; although it called clearly, it looked more Snipe-like as it flew overhead. Later, I discovered that several wader species occasionally fly with their long legs tucked forward, as Lars Jonsson described in a note in *British Birds* magazine. There are two other August records of Spotted Redshank actually feeding along the stream, one of which stayed for four days in 1981. A newly rolled field, looking just like a dry mudflat, that same autumn, attracted a Ringed Plover, which remained for most of the day. Four more had flown over in September 1975. More regular are the Green Sandpipers, three or four often being present along the stream.

A thick mist hung over the farm on 8th August 1981, when a Sandwich Tern called. It eventually appeared and almost alighted with a flock of Black-headed Gulls before flying off east. A flock of 16 Common Terns flew west in August 1980, while a Kittiwake flew southwest in 1978, also in August.

Turtle Doves quite often form flocks, where there is suitable food, before embarking on their southerly migration. The peak autumn count at the farm concerned 53 in August 1975. Migrant passerines that occur fairly regularly in August and September are Tree Pipit, Yellow Wagtail, Wheatear and Pied Flycatcher. Redstarts are less frequently recorded, while both Nightingale and Wood Warbler have been recorded just twice in the autumn. In 1977 another Red-backed Shrike was present from 20th August to 12th September – a memorable year for Shrikes.

A Hobby was seen on four dates in August 1981, but they are more often seen in September, during which month they have occurred in five different years.

As in the spring, one can sometimes be lucky to witness a fall of migrants. Flocks of at least 20 Willow Warblers were present on two dates in August 1979, but of greater interest was a mixed flock of at least 15 Chiffchaffs and Willow Warblers that occurred on 26th September 1976. Three of the latter species showed characteristics of the northern race *P.t.acredula*. A thunderstorm during the night may well have brought down this group of migrants.

Small flocks of finches are a regular feature of the autumn, but in 1976 a field of rape was left unharvested, following the dry summer, and there were minimum estimates of 1,000 Greenfinches and 1,500 Linnets, including an all white, albino individual. These numbers remained until the end of October, when the rape was eventually ploughed in. The finches not only attracted up to four Kestrels and two Hobbys during mid-September, but also the first Merlin to be seen on the farm in mid-October. An exceptionally late Hobby was seen there again on 27th October.

Nuthatches are scarce at Langley, as there is no real woodland, and of the four records, three have been in August and September. Another scarce species, the Cetti's Warbler, was first seen in September 1974.

One of the regular features of September and early October is the southerly passage of *hirundines*. Swallows and House Martins predominate, but small numbers of Sand Martins can also be seen. Counts of 100–200 an hour are not unusual. Flocks of Goldfinches are a colourful sight and concentrations of 100–150 have occasionally gathered at this time, but they invariably disperse by early November.

The departure dates of summer migrants are another interesting aspect of a local study and by the end of September a number will have flown south. The latest recorded dates, in brackets, and the mean departure dates are as follows:

Cuckoo	29 Aug.	(3/10)	Spotted Flycatcher	29 Sept.	(10/10)
Garden Warbler	7 Sept.	(16/9)	Blackcap	29 Sept.	(12/10)
Swift	16 Sept.	(19/10)	Reed Warbler	29 Sept.	(14/11)
Willow Warbler	17 Sept.	(3/10)	Whinchat	4 Oct.	(27/10)
Whitethroat	20 Sept.	(7/10)	Turtle Dove	4 Oct.	(27/10)
Lesser					
Whitethroat	21 Sept.	(27/9)	Chiffchaff	12 Oct.	(27/10)
Sedge Warbler	23 Sept.	(7/10)	House Martin	22 Oct.	(11/11)
Sand Martin	24 Sept.	(11/10)	Swallow	23 Oct.	(1/11)
Wheatear	29 Sept.	(14/10)			

An analysis of the departure dates shows that the autumn of 1976 was quite remarkable for the number of species that were seen later than in any other year. A total of nine in fact, with one being quite exceptional, the Reed Warbler on 14th November. At the time there was only one other later date on record for the British Isles. Such was the influence of the long, hot summer and unusually mild autumn.

October can also be a very exciting month, when much change takes place. Overnight frosts and cold northerly winds often remind one that winter is not far off, but in other years, warm spells help to postpone those thoughts. Large flocks of Lapwings gather in the fields, several hundred Black-headed Gulls can be expected to follow the plough, while westerly movements of migrants from the Continent may involve Chaffinches, Bramblings and quite large flocks of Starlings. On occasions they descend into the hop gardens, before flying to a nearby roost. With several thousand birds involved, it can be an impressive sight.

Fieldfares and Redwings are regular autumn migrants and winter visitors and their mean arrival dates, with the earliest in brackets, are as follows:

Fieldfare   6 October   (13/9)   Redwing   8 October   (4/10)

Increases in the numbers of Song Thrushes, Blackbirds and even Goldcrests are a further indication of influxes from the Continent. Jays may also feature, with small flocks moving through, or sometimes flying over high, as in October 1975, when a total of 24 flew southeast. Meadow Pipits too move south at this time, with small flocks occasionally staying to feed, while Skylark numbers increase, as they form into flocks of up to 100 or more.

The status of the Stonechat has varied considerably, but it became an almost annual autumn migrant and winter visitor between 1974–78. Black Redstarts have occurred in just three autumns, between 11th–19th October. Single Ring Ouzels have also been seen in just three autumns. Another interesting autumn migrant is the Bearded Tit. One to five have been seen in eight different years, five of the records occurring between 18th–24th October and the other three between 2nd–20th November. One of the earliest records involved a bird that had been colour-ringed as an adult at Minsmere in the summer of that year.

The first Barn Owl on the farm was present from 1st October into December 1975. Among the other October rarities are a male Crossbill in 1979, three Mealy Redpolls in 1975, and two Buzzards, one each in 1975 and 1976.

November–December
It may remain mild during November and December, but it is more likely to be unsettled, with periods of heavy rain, or strong winds, severe frosts, or occasional snow.

Another overland migrant in recent years has been the Brent Goose, particularly during northeasterly winds at the end of October or in early November. Flocks have been seen in four autumns, with a maximum of 230 flying south on 29th October 1981. In early November 1975 two flocks, totalling 210, flew southwest in northeasterly gales, to be followed by four Curlews and an arrival of about 200 Fieldfares.

Duck species such as Gadwall, Wigeon and Shoveler, Pochard and, on two occasions, Goldeneye have also occurred, but usually making just brief visits to the lake. Another Merlin was seen in November 1979. The first Short-eared Owl on the farm was first seen on 15th December 1976, remaining to winter, while a roost of 10 Long-eared Owls was discovered in November 1975.

The Great Grey Shrike is another scarce visitor that has occurred at this time in four autumns, arriving between 28th October and 16th November, with a memorable occasion on 18th November 1972, when two were not only seen together, but were heard calling.

Two other quite unexpected rarities deserve mention. Single Snow Buntings were seen in November 1973 and December 1978, with a Lapland Bunting in December 1971.

During the early part of the winter, the flocks of Lapwings may increase to several hundred birds, with a peak of 1,200 in November 1980. Jack Snipe and Woodcock can be disturbed occasionally. The reedbed provides a roost for Pied Wagtails in some winters, though they seem to prefer the warmth of the nearby industrial estate. There were up to 70 in November 1979. The flocks of Fieldfares may number several hundred birds, even a thousand on occasions, but Redwing numbers rarely exceed 100 at this time and frequently decline to 10 or 20 during December. The flock of Skylarks occasionally continues to increase, with a peak of two flocks of 250 and 75 in December 1978.

One of the most impressive cold weather movements occurred, fittingly, on the last day of the year in 1978, when in blizzard conditions a flock of 28 White-fronted Geese, the first to be seen over Langley, flew northwest, over 1,000 Lapwings flew south, totals of 70 Great Black-backed and 32 Herring Gulls flew southeast, and at least 200 Skylarks flew west.

With such a variety of interest, I hope I have shown why working your own patch can be so fascinating and rewarding. My only regret is that I was not able to live there. I wonder what more I might have gained from making daily observations?

As I conclude the writing of this book, Bob and I are now looking forward to studying a new local patch, involving Boughton Park and the adjacent farm, where a new reservoir is being constructed. We are already getting quite excited by the prospect and envisage that this new area will be even more productive than Langley Park Farm.

May Days

How many different species is it possible to record in one day?

I suppose I have always been aware of the fascination that this particular question poses and I well remember in August 1955 being very pleased with a total of 83 species at Cley, Norfolk. But it was not until I spent two years in Canada that I really took up the challenge with any seriousness. There, on 11th May 1963 at Point Pelee, I managed to see 135 different species, and believe it or not 55 of them were then new life species! The following May I again recorded over 130.

Since returning to England in the summer of 1964 and settling in Kent, the May Day outing has become an annual event, shared with first one and now two regular companions. The first trip, rather coincidentally, occurred on 13th May 1965, on which date David Pearson, in Suffolk, achieved his best total, at that time, of 126 species, which he has written up in *The Bird Watchers' Book* edited by John Gooders. On that day we only achieved a modest 102. Since then a little more thought has gone into the planning of a suitable route and in all but two years we have achieved higher totals than that. The cumulative total of 181 different species, over twenty years, gives some indication of the variety of species that occur in Kent during May.

I have often considered other months of the year. An autumn date, coinciding with a good fall of migrants at one of the coastal Observatories, would almost certainly produce over 100 species, but to exceed 120, or 130, I am sure that mid-May is the best period. One important factor is the abundance of bird song at this time, by which many of the resident and migrant breeding species are located.

In planning such a trip it is vital to establish, beforehand, if you can, the precise location of some of our more difficult breeding species, such as the Long-eared Owl and Woodcock. The latter, rather surprisingly, did not appear on our May Day list until 1983! We tend to drive over two hundred miles during the day, visiting a wide variety of habitats to produce those extra few species. East Kent probably offers the best opportunities for an unmotorised May Day, visiting the Stour Valley, Sandwich Bay and possibly a cliff site for a seawatch, but I am not sufficiently familiar with that part of the county to concentrate my May Day attempts there.

Ideally, the weather needs to be fine and dry with little or no wind to restrict the bird song, and if Dungeness is included in the itinerary, then the tide needs to be fairly low, when seabirds are attracted to the 'patch'.

The weather for our first May Day was gloriously hot. A Wryneck called near Aylesford, a Wood Warbler sang his beautiful liquid notes from the beeches at Detling, and Capel Fleet produced a splendid variety of passage waders, including Whimbrel, Spotted Redshank, Ruff and Wood Sandpiper. Returning to Aylesford after dark, we heard a Quail calling. In other years rain has severely limited our success, though it has never prevented our totalling over 100 species. On 4th May 1971 we saw a number of late wintering birds, including a Pink-footed Goose at Lade Pits, a pair of Long-tailed Ducks and a Brent Goose at the ARC pit at Dungeness and a Wigeon on Capel Fleet. The comparison of dawn chorus species over the years is quite fascinating. The Nightingale has always appeared in the top three and in 1974 we heard a Swallow singing as early as 0334.

Pride of place must surely go to the Laughing Gull, an American species seen on 11th May 1966, which at that time was the first to be accepted for the British Isles.

On 14th May 1978 we eventually achieved what seemed then to be a magical total of 120. It was overcast when we set out, but still, with light rain which ceased shortly after dawn. There were some breaks in the cloud early on, but the wind got up and increased to fresh SW, with squally showers during the afternoon. However, the evening was fine, with clear skies and no wind.

We left East Sutton at 0230. Neither Tawny nor Little Owls were calling in the miserably damp conditions. During a brief stop at 0320 near Harbledown we heard our first species, a Nightingale, followed shortly by a Robin. The other side of Canterbury we stopped again, by the golf course, and heard the first of a number of Cetti's Warblers singing.

In Trenley Park Woods, opposite Westbere, we added 40 species in the next two hours. Some time after 0330 Coot, Woodpigeon and Little Owl were heard calling. Shortly after 0415 the dawn chorus commenced quite suddenly and we heard the songs or calls of Skylark, Blackbird, Dunnock, Song Thrush, Willow Warbler, Yellowhammer, Reed Bunting and Sedge Warbler in quick succession, followed by Moorhen, Cuckoo, Blackcap, Wren, Mistle Thrush and Reed Warbler. Through the dim light of dawn we could just make out Mallard and Great Crested Grebe swimming close to the reeds. A Rook called in the distance, while in the alders Blue and Great Tits were calling, a Garden Warbler sang and a Turtle Dove purred. From across the water the startled cry of a Canada Goose preceded the deep croak of a Carrion Crow. As the light improved both Mute Swan and Greylag Goose came into view and a Pheasant called. Two not dissimilar calls were then heard, the first a harsh 'tchick' from a Great Spotted Woodpecker, a species we have missed on several occasions, then several 'tchaks' as a Jackdaw flew by. It was now after 0500 and the light was improving rapidly. Sand Martins were flying to and from the Trenley Park sand pit, a Chaffinch and a Starling flew amongst the trees. The next species, a Jay, is one we always like to record early on, as it too had been missed completely on one May Day trip. Tree Sparrow and Linnet were quickly added as we drove down towards Stodmarsh and in the village itself we saw a Collared Dove.

A Whitethroat was singing as we arrived in the Stodmarsh car park at 0530 and Goldfinches flew up from the pools of water along the path, where they had been drinking. We rely on Stodmarsh to produce a good variety of species, but in particular certain rather specialised birds that we are unlikely to see anywhere else on our chosen route. The first of these, the Bearded Tit, was quickly added, as several of them called and flitted from reed to reed alongside the Lampen Wall. The drumming of a Snipe was another welcome sound. Shoveler, Swallow, Pochard and a House Sparrow were then seen and at 0540 our 50th species, an attractive drake Teal, swam out from the reeds.

A Redpoll called as it flew over, Tufted Duck and Shelduck could be seen on the water, and a distinctive reeling song attracted us to another Stodmarsh speciality, the Savi's Warbler, which continued to sing from a reed stem as we watched it closely. A Redshank called clearly as it flew low over the Lampen Wall, while high overhead the first Swift appeared. As we continued along the wall several Greenfinches, a lone Cormorant, a Herring Gull and a few Black-headed Gulls flew over. By 0600 we had ticked off 60 species.

In the fields across the Stour a pair of Grey Partridge was feeding, while a Water Rail squealed from the reeds behind us. This was a welcome bonus, as we have only recorded this species on three other May Days. A pair of Garganey and several Meadow Pipits flew up from the marshy fields, a Great Black-backed Gull flew overhead and the rattle-like song of a Lesser Whitethroat burst from a group of hawthorns. House Martins then appeared, flying low over the Stour and a Common Sandpiper was disturbed from the river bank.

By now it was 0630 and we were close to Grove Ferry. A Stock Dove and a Grey Heron flew over, while on the short grass of the turf fields we could see several Ringed Plovers, but there was no sign of the Little Ringed Plovers that had been seen there earlier in the week. Walking back along the river bank we were happy to hear the more metallic reeling of a Grasshopper Warbler, another species we have had some difficulty recording in recent years.

Although not entirely unexpected, as it had been first seen the previous day, the presence of a Pallid Swift was an exceptional bonus and we spent about twenty minutes studying it closely. The light was not brilliant, but the sun was breaking through the early morning cloud and viewing conditions, particularly as the bird flew low over the Lampen Wall, frequently against a background of trees, were quite adequate. This individual was the first to be satisfactorily identified in Britain.

No Bitterns had boomed and we had not seen Gadwall or the Glossy Ibis – though I heard later that it had flown over our heads as we had been watching the Pallid Swift! However, we left Stodmarsh at 0825 feeling well satisfied with our 75 species and particularly elated over the Pallid Swift, a remarkably obliging bird.

A number of woodland species were still missing and if they are not found early in the morning many fruitless hours could be wasted later in the day. *En route* to Church Wood we glimpsed a Bullfinch and our first Magpie. During the next hour, although we failed to find any Redstarts or Wood Warblers, which were supposed to be present, we did add a number of the more difficult species, including Green Woodpecker, Willow Tit, Nuthatch, Tree Pipit, Coal Tit – missed on two previous trips – Chiffchaff, Treecreeper and Goldcrest.

Along the Thanet Way *en route* to Minnis Bay we saw Corn Bunting and Red-legged Partridge, both perched on fence posts! Arriving at Minnis Bay at 1040 we added Pied Wagtail and Wheatear and our 90th species, a Stonechat, the bird we had particularly hoped to see here. A migrant Whinchat was also present and along the shore we saw Turnstone, Oystercatcher and Little Tern.

A Kestrel, another species that has been difficult to find on past occasions, was perched on the Church in Birchington. At Foreness Point around 1135 we quickly added Fulmar, a lone Common Scoter and the summering flock of Eider.

The tide was right out as we drove down to Pegwell Bay and the waders were too distant to identify with any certainty. With a rising tide we might well have added several wader species, including Curlew and Knot, which we failed to find later in the day.

We left Sandwich at around noon and found the drive south quite tiring, eventually arriving at Lade Sands at 1335, where we soon saw four Bar-tailed Godwits and a small flock of Sanderling, our 100th species. Several Dunlin were also feeding at the water's edge. At Lade Pits we saw Common and Lesser Black-backed Gulls, but failed to find the expected Little Grebes. Was this species going to be our bogey bird this year? Inevitably one or more common species elude us.

At Dungeness Bird Observatory we found a Black Redstart in the moat, but the trapping area was apparently quiet and we decided to concentrate our efforts on a seawatch, which we commenced at 1415. A Manx Shearwater had flown by just ten minutes earlier, but undismayed we spent the next ninety minutes adding a number of useful species, including Common and Sandwich Terns, one definite Red-throated Diver out of a total of ten divers, at least 20 Gannets, an immature Kittiwake, three Razorbills and a Guillemot. Soon after we left an Arctic Skua apparently flew up-Channel, but nevertheless it had been quite a productive period, increasing our day's total to 112 species.

At Burrowe's Pit, on the RSPB Reserve, we saw a Ruff and a Whimbrel, but failed to find any Black Terns or Little Gulls, two species that frequently occur here in the spring. We left at 1715, returning to East Sutton just after 1800, where we were fortunate enough to find a Hawfinch, our 115th species.

Several woodland species were still missing and we had not seen or heard a Little Grebe, so we put our faith in a small section of the Len Valley at Broomfield. Here, shortly before 1900, we located a pair of Long-tailed Tits and a Marsh Tit, both species we have failed to find on previous May Days. A little later we had the pleasure of watching a pair of Kingfishers chasing each other up and down the stream. There was no sign of the Grey Wagtails which I normally expect to see here, but a Spotted Flycatcher was busy flying to and from its perch on a dead alder.

At 2020 I eventually glimpsed a Little Grebe as it dived below the lake's surface. It gave me an immensely satisfying feeling to achieve at long last my target of 120 species in a day in Kent. It had taken fifteen attempts and, although on paper there seemed to be ample species in the county at that time, it had proved to be a considerable task.

You may or may not allow me to add the Mandarin which appeared a short while later. This species does breed in the wild here, but they are quite a common duck at the Leeds wildfowl collection just a short way down the valley.

The evening was still and clear and I had every hope of adding Woodcock and possibly even Nightjar in the nearby chestnut coppiced area of Kingswood, but it was not to be. Sadly, the latter species seems to have disappeared from this area. As the last of the evening light faded, I considered it a most pleasant end to a memorable day.

In more recent years, with the increased interest in May Day Birdwatches (see *The Big Bird Race* by Bill Oddie and David Tomlinson) and the fund-raising potential they have, I began to look at our efforts even more critically. In planning our route for 16th May 1982, I came to the conclusion that visiting woodland in south Kent, before doing an early morning seawatch at Dungeness, might well make a more worthwhile start.

It was still, with a cloudless sky, when we visited Challock Forest shortly before 0300, on 16th May 1982. Both Nightjar and Nightingale were performing well as we left for Hamstreet Woods. There, as dawn broke, we quickly added a wide selection of woodland species and we departed around 0600 with 50 species on our list. On the way to Dungeness we visited Dengemarsh and the ARC pit, where a Little Ringed Plover was a welcome bonus. The next hour or so was really rather disappointing. After some good sea passage the previous week, the flat calm and light wind were not conducive to up-Channel movement and we only added six species. There were very few passerine migrants around the Observatory, but brief visits to Lade Sands and Lade Pits, then Burrowe's Pit, eventually produced our 100th species, a Sand Martin at 1030. Lyminge Forest produced the expected Firecrest, followed by two Dotterel at Sandwich Bay, a Whimbrel in Pegwell Bay and Fulmars at Foreness. The highlight of the day was the sighting of an Osprey, as it drifted slowly up the Stour Valley, while Westbere produced four more species, including Savi's Warbler. Arriving at Elmley around 1900, with 117 species already recorded, we added five more duck species and five waders, including the Glossy Ibis; a total of 127 species. The new route had paid off handsomely.

The challenge now was to see 130 species. Another change was considered for 1984 – to start at midnight. For various reasons May 6th was selected, but the darkness of the heavily cloud covered night sky and the cold, quite strong NE wind prevented us hearing as much as we had hoped for in the Stour Valley. However, a Savi's Warbler did sing well for us. Dawn was exceedingly slow in breaking over Fagg's Wood and though we ticked off Woodcock before 0430, the dawn chorus did not get underway until fifteen minutes later. Sadly, the Crossbills that were present still had not appeared when we left at 0600, but Hamstreet Woods again produced a good selection of woodland specialities, including Hawfinch and Lesser Spotted Woodpecker. We had totalled 56 when we left there just after 0700, about an hour behind schedule. The seawatch commenced at 0800, by which time we had recorded 82 species, but it too was disappointing and we only added six more, including Gannet and Arctic Tern – no sign of any divers, skuas or auks, not even a Kittiwake or Common Scoter. The trapping area was also fairly quiet, although a Golden Oriole had been seen that morning. We quickly added Stonechat, Wheatear and Black Redstart, and Common Sandpiper on the Long Pits, while a little more time at the ARC pit produced a lone Sand Martin – our only one of the day – and a Little Ringed Plover, but there was no sign of the Temminck's Stint that had been seen there. We were now well behind our schedule and cursing the strong wind.

Suddenly, for some inexplicable reason, our luck seemed to change as we looked out to sea off the Brooks. We chose to go there primarily to see Eider, and as we scanned the water at 1100 we saw a fine Slavonian Grebe in breeding plumage, our 100th species. Five more species then followed in quick succession, including the Eider, Velvet Scoter and Red-breasted Merganser. Although we had left the Dungeness area by this time in 1982, it was noon before we reached 105 in that year. Our expectations took on a new look, particularly when we added five more species at the Burrowe's Pit, including a Black-necked Grebe, though we failed to see the Mediterranean Gulls that were there. Back to the ARC pit yet again and this time we found the Temminck's Stint and we were able to leave the Dungeness area, ticking off Knot on Lade Sands as our 112th species, at 1300.

From there on everything seemed to fall into place as planned, apart from a slight hiccup when we failed to stop at Sandling Park to try for that increasingly elusive Bullfinch – we never did find one! Several Firecrests were either calling or singing in Lyminge Forest at 1350 and we decided not to spend time searching for Crossbills there, but drove on to Pegwell Bay by 1430, where we added Curlew and two more unexpected bonuses – Brent Goose and Avocet. The adrenalin was really beginning to flow.

Now that Ring-necked Parakeet is on the British list as a feral breeder, we visited Port Regis and quickly located a pair, before moving on to Foreness Point to find the Purple Sandpipers roosting on the tideline. A brief visit to Westbere around 1645 produced Bearded Tit, but we did not stay long enough to hear Snipe or Water Rail. The Canterbury Grey Wagtail could not have been more obliging and forty minutes later we were on Sheppey and looking at a Marsh Harrier. As we drove down towards the Elmley Reserve at 1800, with 122 species already listed, we felt confident that we could exceed the target of 130 for the first time.

The Dotterel, which had been there for some time, were most obligingly still present, a pair of Grey Partridge appeared at last and several Whimbrel called as they flew off. On the floods we added four duck species and three more waders, bringing the total to 132 by 1930. Two known localities in central Kent produced Long-eared Owl and Barn Owl respectively, just before 2100. A marvellous climax to a superb day's birdwatching. A total of 134 species had exceeded our highest expectations, and yet, as always, we had missed quite a number of common species.

Looking back over the years, it is interesting to note some of the changes that have occurred. We failed to record Redpoll at all until 1970, but since then we have had no difficulty in seeing it annually. Its spread as a breeding species in recent years has been quite remarkable. Similarly, the Cetti's Warbler has become a regular since 1973. On the debit side we no longer record Wryneck, which has almost certainly ceased to breed in Kent, and rarely see or hear Wood Warbler, which has become a scarce breeding bird in this county.

I wonder what the future holds? Now that we seem to have a good route established, can we expect, with the right weather conditions and the correct tides, to top 140 species?

A Year in Kent – 1977

Many birdwatchers keep annual lists and I have often wondered how many different species I could satisfactorily identify in Kent during a calendar year. On average 256 species are recorded annually in this county, with a range of 242–267 during 1970–82. Of these, 207 species have been seen in every year. A total of 200, therefore, should not be too difficult to exceed, so I made a special effort during 1977 to achieve that target.

It obviously entails quite a lot of travelling around the county, particularly during the migration seasons. Being on the 'grape vine' too is probably essential to catch up with sufficient accidental visitors, so I spread word of my intentions.

For many years I have endeavoured to start the year well with a good variety of species on New Year's Day. Since living in Kent, I have in fact recorded 146 different species on 1st January and exceeded 100 on three of the ten occasions when I have spent all the daylight hours in the field. My best total to date is the 109 recorded in 1982.

With two fellow enthusiasts I prepared more carefully than usual for our 1st January 1977 trip.

January 1st A moderate wind blew from the SW as dawn broke and the Little Owls I had expected to hear were not calling. We spent an hour or so at my local patch near Maidstone, hoping in particular to record Water Rail, Jack Snipe, Grey Wagtail and Willow Tit, in addition to the Little Owl. By 0815 we had noted 38 species, but only two of the five specialities, Water Rail and Willow Tit, were included.

The previous day we had located a roost of Long-eared Owls in nearby Kingswood, so the next stop found us trampling through fern and bramble covered undergrowth in a small conifer plantation. The Long-eared Owls were still present and although we did not flush a Woodcock, as we had the previous day, we did manage to add Jay, Coal

Tit, Marsh Tit and Green Woodpecker, all in the space of fifteen minutes.

The next hour, in damp conditions, was spent at Mote Park, where we heard and glimpsed a Cetti's Warbler, saw a duck Goosander and a Ruddy Duck on the lake and also added Kingfisher and Treecreeper, two species that can be difficult to locate on this type of day. For the first time that I can remember there was no sign of any wintering Siskins feeding in the alders; in their place were flocks of Goldfinches. When we left Mote Park at 0945 the total had risen to 58 species.

On the way to the Medway Estuary we added Magpie and Collared Dove. Fortunately as we drove down to Lower Halstow, it was close to high tide and a good variety of species, with waders in particular, were roosting on the grassy slopes above Halstow Creek. We quickly added nine species in as many minutes, including Grey Plover, Ringed Plover, Wigeon, Brent Goose and Cormorant. We then stopped, overlooking Barksore, by which time the weather was being far kinder. The sun shone brightly as we looked over the marshes and saw literally thousands of wildfowl and waders. It was a magnificent spectacle. A skein of about a hundred White-fronted Geese flew in from the NE to join the several hundred Brent Geese and small flock of Greylags already grazing there. Large numbers of Wigeon kept winging their way to and fro and a sizeable flock of Pintail added a touch of elegance to the scene. Among the Golden Plover running over the fields close to the road were three Black-tailed Godwits, a relatively rare species in winter.

It was by now 1050 and the total had increased to 76. We scanned Funton Creek very thoroughly, but failed to locate any Red-breasted Mergansers.

A half hour drive took us to Shellness on the Isle of Sheppey, where the strength of the SW wind had increased considerably. Another eight species were added during the hour we spent there. Oystercatcher, Knot and Bar-tailed Godwit were quickly located and we were fortunate enough to find the Purple Sandpiper, which was wintering there with the Turnstones. A flock of Snow Buntings was present on the shingle spit, as expected, and in the strong wind they flew even more erratically, with their white wing patches looking like wind-blown scraps of paper against the darkening sky. Short-eared Owls can usually be seen here, but were not present in good numbers this winter.

A lunch stop at Capel Fleet was pleasingly productive, despite some more heavy rain. A pair of Stonechats perched momentarily on a fence close to the car before dropping to the ground to feed. There was a flock of about forty swans sitting in the winter wheat some three hundred metres distant and when the rain ceased I scanned through them, using my telescope. As I had wishfully thought, though not really expected, in amongst the Mute Swans were about a dozen adult Bewick's. Finally, in the distance, I picked out an adult male Hen Harrier gliding gracefully along a drainage ditch.

We left Capel Fleet for Cliffe Pools at 1315, stopping at Funton Creek again, still hoping to add Red-breasted Merganser, but only finding Little Grebe and Goldeneye to bring the day's total to 89.

Arriving at Cliffe around 1430, we quickly found a pair of Scaup and some Shoveler, but failed to see the Long-tailed Duck that was wintering there. However, the hour and a half before dusk was quite productive and between us we added Snipe, Jack Snipe, Lesser Black-backed Gull, Twite, Short-eared Owl and Red-necked Grebe. This final flourish brought the total for the day to 97 and my own to 96, as I had missed the Short-eared Owl.

January 2nd The weather was foul, but in the morning I did manage to add three species that we had missed the day before. A covey of Red-legged Partridges was eventually discovered within a few hundred metres of my home and later I saw both Long-tailed Tits and Nuthatches. It was not until eleven o'clock that evening that I ticked off the 100th species, when a Little Owl deigned to call at long last.

January 3rd Both Great Spotted and Lesser Spotted Woodpeckers obligingly appeared on my local patch and a further visit to Cliffe produced the Long-tailed Duck and a few Ruff, the second group of which were feeding on the flooded cricket square at Cooling!

January 4th The first of many trips to Dungeness was made, essentially to see the Smew that were wintering there. The various gravel pits in the area attract a good variety of wildfowl in the winter months and on this visit I added four more species, a lone Pink-footed Goose, several Gadwall, a nice drake Common Scoter and three 'red-headed' Smew. In the Observatory area I failed to find the wintering Chiffchaff, but did flush my first Woodcock of the year. Towards the end of the day I visited Langley again. I flushed another Woodcock and re-discovered the Short-eared Owl, that I had first seen there in mid-December. The year's total had risen to 110.

January 6th A trip to east Kent failed to produce some of the rarer species I had hoped to see, like Shore Lark, Lapland Bunting and the wintering Avocets, but I did add Red-throated Diver on Stonar Lake, and several Bearded Tits and a Bittern at Stodmarsh. I saw this bird a mere five metres away, feeding along the edge of a ditch. It put on a masterly reed-feigning act. A snatch of Cetti's song momentarily drew my attention away and when I looked back all I could see was a 'broken reed'. On walking a little closer, however, the 'reed' straightened a fraction and as I walked past the Bittern smoothly pivoted its head and neck, keeping me at the same angle all the time.

January 9th Every winter produces slight variations to the usual pattern of events. This winter was not to be an exception. I have already mentioned the scarcity of Siskins. Bramblings, too, were scarce and as I had not heard of any wintering Great Grey Shrikes it was a most pleasurable moment when one suddenly appeared in my binocular vision. At the time, I was studying a Short-eared Owl sitting on the plough, again at Langley.

January 11th The Grey Wagtail was missing from the year's list until now, when one flew over Pudding Lane, Maidstone, calling distinctly as it disappeared over the rooftops.

January 14th I shall inevitably use the description 'rarity' when referring to some species. To give the term some measure of qualification I shall refer to those species that have not occurred annually since 1970 as 'rarities'.

The first such species was seen when, following a few enquiries, I located a Dipper in the Loose Valley. Apparently quite a creature of habit, it came to roost at the same spot each evening. As one would expect, it was a Continental bird of the black-bellied race *C.c.cinclus*. In the same valley a Cetti's Warbler was calling frequently, occasionally providing me with quite excellent, close views. Kingfishers were seen quite easily and all three woodpeckers were present, but I did not find any Hawfinches, though they certainly occur here regularly.

January 16th I visited Bedgebury Pinetum, in the late afternoon, to see the Hawfinches which regularly roost here during the winter months. The numbers were difficult to estimate, but certainly fifty, possibly many more, were present. There was no sign of the usual Bramblings that also roost here, but I did have the good fortune to see an adult male Hen Harrier sailing over the forest to the southwest.

January 18th A single Brambling at Langley brought the year's total to 118.

January 23rd Another trip into east Kent, this time visiting Thanet as well as the Stour Valley. Rumours of a small crake species took me into the Stour Valley near Chartham, but without much hope as these creatures are particularly skulking in their habits. A search for a Shore Lark near Minnis Bay also proved fruitless, but I did manage to add Sanderling at last. At Foreness Point a flock of twelve Eiders was feeding offshore and a group of fourteen Purple Sandpipers perched briefly on a groyne, before the incoming tide rose over it. Two Fulmars also flew past. Close to Grove Ferry I heard a Green Sandpiper calling and later flushed a second bird. This species is wintering more commonly in the county in recent years. At Stodmarsh I recorded my second rarity, when I had distant views of a Glossy Ibis as it flew in to roost. This individual had been present in this area for a year or so. A number of Cetti's Warblers were in song and two Hen Harriers obligingly flew close, low over the reeds as dusk descended. I was hoping to catch a glimpse of a Merlin that was wintering here, but it was not to be on this occasion.

January 30th A visit into west Kent produced nothing new, but at Bough Beech reservoir a pair of Ruddy Ducks, a drake Goosander and an *aythya* hybrid were present. The latter provided excellent, close views enabling detailed notes to be taken, showing that it was probably a hybrid Pochard X Tufted Duck. On the Sevenoaks Reserve I also had excellent views of a feral Bean Goose of the 'Tundra' race *A.f.rossicus*, a smaller, shorter necked bird than the 'Forest' race *A.f.fabilis*, which has a short, mainly dark bill and only a small patch of yellowish orange towards the tip. Fine, brown streaks gave the neck a dark appearance.

The total by the end of January had reached 123. Siskins remained elusive and of the other regular species that might have been recorded only Red-breasted Merganser, Sparrowhawk, Merlin, Barn and Tawny Owl were missing.

February was exceptionally mild and very wet and I heard of little to attract me from my local study area, where on one occasion I enjoyed a staring match with the wintering Short-eared Owl. What fascinating creatures they are with their large, round, yellow eyes.

February 13th Reports of Bean Geese and Avocets wintering on the Isle of Sheppey tempted me to visit that area. The weather was fair and fine views of an adult male Hen Harrier once again near Capel Fleet got the day off to a good start. The numbers of Lapwings present created an impressive spectacle when they were disturbed. Before long I was fortunate enough to locate the Bean Geese standing in an area of ploughed land. These five were of the 'Forest' race that regularly winter in Britain. A larger, longer necked bird than the 'Tundra' Bean, the dark head and neck contrasting with paler underparts. Later I saw them in flight and also with White-fronted Geese, which offered valuable size and plumage comparisons.

There were large numbers of duck along Capel Fleet, including thirty to forty Gadwall, an unusually high number for this locality. The next new species for the year's list was a Spotted Redshank and at least three were seen during the day. Two Hooded Crows, considered a subspecies of the Carrion Crow by most authorities, appeared around mid-day, but the afternoon belonged to the geese.

Several skeins of White-fronts stretched across the sky and a total of six hundred would be a fairly conservative estimate. Some two hundred of these came in to feed, eventually allowing quite close approach, a delightful sight in the low afternoon sun. To the south over the Swale a large skein of about four hundred Brent Geese were calling noisily as they dropped in to feed on the winter wheat.

No Avocets could be found, nor Merlin, but, just as I was leaving at dusk, an obliging Barn Owl floated over the road and flew along the fleet.

February 17th Rumours of a Red-crested Pochard at Bewl Bridge Reservoir on the Kent/Sussex border tempted me to visit this huge, new inland expanse of water. Unfortunately the weather was foul and it rained heavily most of the time I was there. Though I scanned through large numbers of Pochard, my only find of particular note was three Scaup. However, the visit was not without some reward as I was able to study a delightful, small goose known as the Cackling Canada Goose *B.c.minima*, a half-size subspecies of the familiar Canada Goose with which it was feeding, with a much smaller bill, a comparatively large white face patch and a white ring at the base of the neck. Its origin must remain open to speculation, but apparently quite a number are kept in captivity.

February 24th On my local study area, as is usual in late February and early March, Redwings were gathering before moving north to their breeding grounds. From the flocks one can frequently hear a murmur of subsong, but less often an individual may break into full flow; the day was particularly spring-like and I was treated to several bursts of this most attractive song.

February 27th Back into north Kent in comparatively cold conditions, following a severe overnight frost, I found the pools at Cliffe contained surprisingly few duck, but a brief neck stretching display by a drake Goldeneye was a rewarding sight.

It never ceased to amaze me how incredibly pink was the Greater Flamingo which resided here until 1980. Presumably it found an adequate supply of suitable food to maintain its brilliant colour. Though somewhat incongruous in this setting, it was nevertheless a magnificent spectacle.

At Northward Hill many of the Grey Herons were back at their nests. It is the largest heronry in the British Isles. At Grain a drake Long-tailed Duck and five Scaup could be seen well, amongst a party of Pochard and Tufted Duck, in a roadside lagoon. At Funton Creek and Barksore the large numbers of duck were again a most impressive sight. Here, by diligent scanning, I was at last able to add Red-breasted Merganser to the year's list. A single pair was swimming and diving in a distant creek.

March 6th Reports of a Buzzard at the Tunbridge Wells rubbish tip took me to that locality, but with little hope of success. This species is relatively difficult to see with any certainty in Kent. As expected, I failed to find it, but the visit did not pass without some reward. It is well to remember that rubbish tips can attract some interesting species. This afternoon there were over two hundred Carrion Crows present and amongst them a single Hooded Crow.

March 9th An exceptionally warm, spring-like day and I managed a brief visit to Langley. In one small area I saw three different butterfly species, a Peacock, a Brimstone and a Comma. The previous day I had seen a Small Tortoiseshell. To add a further taste of spring quite a number of toads were croaking and others mating, but the most pleasant spectacle for my eyes was the presence of an early Chiffchaff, which obligingly uttered a single phrase of song, though it seemed more concerned with preening and feeding low down in brambles and reeds. As with all species which occasionally overwinter, one can never be sure whether the early ones you see are genuine spring migrants. This bird, too, had a rather dark plumage, with a suggestion of brownish underparts, indicating that it might possibly be one of the northern races and more likely to be overwintering. However, this failed to detract from the pleasurable experience of an early breath of spring.

March 13th Another visit to Langley produced further signs of spring. A flock of about fifty Redpolls was feeding among the new buds of willow saplings. Until now only three or four had been seen. The Chiffchaff was still present in the same patch of reeds, but more exciting was the presence of a pair of Wheatears on a newly-ploughed field. They were certainly early migrants.

March 22nd Reports of Garganey, Ring Ouzels, Swallows, Sand Martins and a fall of thirty-five Chiffchaffs at Dungeness indicated an early spring, but by today the wind was round in the NE quarter and the weather was far from spring-like. However, I was fortunate enough to see both Black Redstart and Firecrest in the Dungeness Observatory area, the latter almost bursting into full song. Offshore there was little of note, but I did see my first Kittiwake of the year. Burrowe's Pit, on the RSPB Reserve, produced two more species that occur less frequently in the county. I had excellent views of a Great Northern Diver and then, by thoroughly checking all the gulls present, I eventually discovered a second-winter Glaucous Gull, another very useful addition to the year's tally.

March 27th Another trip to Dungeness enabled me to add five more species, but the weather was miserable. A thick mist in the morning cleared for a while after mid-day, but there was little respite from the rain and a promising light easterly wind swung right round to the NW, increasing in strength. A more consistent wind between SW and E at this time of year normally produces a good sea passage, though the previous day over a thousand Common Scoter flew up-Channel, when the wind was NE 4.

During the intermittent breaks in the mist, a steady passage of Meadow Pipits and Linnets could be seen and other passerine migrants were arriving in the trapping area. Here I saw my first Willow Warblers of the year and three Sand Martins. At the ARC pit I was fortunate enough to have excellent views of an adult Mediterranean Gull in immaculate breeding plumage.

On the same pit there were about fifteen Goldeneye and two adult drakes were displaying, at times stretching their necks forward and then throwing them right back so that the nape touched the rump. This species apparently displays quite frequently in its winter quarters.

The seawatching hide overlooking the 'patch' is a great boon in such inclement weather conditions. There was not much sea passage on this occasion, but I did see several adult Gannets and my first Sandwich Terns of the year. Several flocks of Common Scoter and two unidentified divers also flew up-Channel, but I missed a Great Skua that appeared while I broke off for lunch – a fatal relaxation of effort!

By now my annual list had reached a fairly respectable 140, with the majority of the regular summer visitors to come. Having entered like the proverbial lamb, March went out like a lion, with cold northerly winds and snow showers. This change in the weather effectively held up the spring migration, just as it has done in a number of recent springs.

April 3rd–16th These two weeks were spent birdwatching in Majorca, where I encountered more snow! There, too, migration was being delayed by cold northerly winds.

At Dungeness the wind direction in spring is a critical factor for migration and a change to SW after a spell in the N produces a quite rapid reaction, particularly from seabirds. Such conditions on the 16th produced the best seabird movement of the spring, with nearly 200 divers, 5,735 Common Scoter and 1,100 Sandwich Terns. A good variety of other species was also seen, but as I was still *en route* from Majorca I was not able to enjoy the experience.

April 17th–18th At this time of year you can expect to add a few new species practically every day you go out. At Langley I soon added my first Swallows and Blackcaps, followed by House Martins feeding over the lake and a Sedge Warbler singing from the reedbed. I always like to see my first Sedge and Reed Warblers each spring just to check that I have not forgotten their respective songs. While searching for this particular individual I heard the harsh 'tac-tac' of a Ring Ouzel and briefly caught a glimpse of his white gorget, before he was seen off by a hen Blackbird. He had been quite innocently feeding on ivy berries, just a little too close to her nest. As the Ring Ouzel is only a passage migrant in Kent, it is nice to record one early in the year, particularly on your own patch.

April 19th On leaving home for Dungeness again, a Cuckoo was calling, another first for the year. The wind remained in the E all day, failing to swing to the S as forecast and a two-hour seawatch produced only a small number of species, but included ten Great Northern and one Red-throated Diver, three Fulmars, a Gannet, only two Common Scoter, about forty Sandwich Terns, a few Common Terns and one immature Little Gull, over the 'patch'. The last two species were new for the year, as was a Yellow Wagtail on the reserve, where one of two Knot was coming into its attractive red summer dress.

April 20th On this day the annual total reached 150, when I visited Langley again and recorded my earliest ever Reed Warbler, singing sweetly in the reedbed, despite the cold conditions. The following day a cock Whitethroat was back, singing from his usual territory.

April 24th Following a report of up to four Shags at an old flooded chalk pit near Gravesend, I decided it was about time that this species appeared on my Kent list. The day was fine and dry, though a strong westerly wind was blowing. Without any difficulty I found two adult Shags and had excellent views of them swimming and diving for fish. Two of the four remained on this pit until the end of June, a quite exceptional record.

In the scrub surrounding the pit both Nightingale and Lesser Whitethroat were singing.

One of the earliest spring migrants is the Little Ringed Plover and as the first had been seen just a month earlier, it was long overdue for my annual list. A visit to one of the many gravel workings in west Kent soon rectified the situation.

April 27th A visit to Broomfield, along the river Len, produced two or three Turtle Doves singing contentedly, such is the nature of their 'purring' song, and from a small stream I flushed a pair of Mandarins, a species which is now breeding ferally in small numbers in the county.

May 1st On a brief visit to a chestnut coppiced area near Langley, I was able to locate about five Tree Pipits, some performing their attractive, parachuting song-flights.

May 6th My annual 'May Day' produced 113 species, eleven of which were additions to my year's list.

The morning started well at Stodmarsh. Just after 0400, a Bittern boomed clearly and about an hour later we heard the reeling song of the first of three or four Savi's Warblers, two of which were seen extremely well at close range, looking very dark against the morning light. The next species, a Marsh Harrier, is being recorded more regularly in Kent in recent years, though I had only seen it once before. The hen bird afforded us good views as it hunted over the reedbeds and at one point she flushed a drake Garganey, another new species for the year. Shortly before 0600 we witnessed a most attractive spectacle as the Glossy Ibis flew across the glowing morning sun several times, before dropping into the fields to feed. It is a strange looking creature, with its long outstretched legs and neck further accentuated by the long decurved bill. It was surprisingly agile in avoiding molesting Lapwings, as it dropped rapidly out of the sky. The only other addition to the year's list at this locality was a Garden Warbler, that most nondescript of species.

A short way down the valley we found the fields at Grove Ferry nicely flooded, providing an attractive feeding ground for migrant freshwater waders. That morning we were most fortunate to find a flock of five Wood Sandpipers. Overhead a number of Swifts were feeding hungrily.

Sometime later in the morning, at Dungeness, I found a Common Sandpiper and also saw an attractive cock Whinchat. An hour and a half long seawatch proved to be quite productive, with nine new species for the day's list and three more for the year. The Little Tern, shortly before 1300, was the 100th species for the day and the 166th for the year. Soon afterwards I was able to identify an Arctic Tern, and a dark-phase Arctic Skua flew close enough to reveal clearly its tail structure.

May 7th I had missed a Hobby at Broomfield by about a minute the previous day, and it did not appear when I visited the area again. However, a Spotted Flycatcher was actively feeding over the pond and I had another good view of the drake Mandarin.

May 15th Reports of three Kentish Plovers and two Avocets at Sandwich Bay, supported by the promise of an easterly wind, took me there early in the day, but, as frequently happens, the birds had flown. I was able to enjoy some fine views of Knot and Grey Plover in their resplendent summer plumages and also managed to add a Greenshank to the year's list.

As the easterly winds had produced nothing of special interest at Sandwich Bay, I decided to visit Dungeness in the afternoon in the hope of seeing some sea passage. Here, too, it was relatively quiet, but on the 'patch' at low tide I was able to enjoy the picturesque sight of about a hundred and fifty terns fishing. The majority were Common Terns, but amongst them were two Black Terns, one of my favourite birds in their smart spring dress. After a while I was also able to identify a Roseate Tern. Although similar in size to the Common, the whiteness of its plumage makes it surprisingly easy to pick out. On this occasion I watched it closely, comparing it with the Common Terns. Its sleeker appearance was obvious, the wings noticeably thinner and the body comparatively long and more slender.

Whenever you specifically set out to see certain species, it seems inevitable that some will continually evade you. This year Tawny Owl and Siskin, Redstart, Grasshopper and Wood Warblers, Whimbrel and Nightjar were all proving extremely elusive. I spent several abortive evenings in late May trying to hear both Nightjar and Grasshopper Warbler. A further visit into east or west Kent would be necessary to see both Redstart and Wood Warbler and surely I would eventually hear a Tawny Owl hooting!

May 29th Into East Kent again with a genuine hope of a rarity or two. A short visit to Church Wood produced the missing Grasshopper Warbler, but there was no sign of either Wood Warbler or Redstart. In the Stour Valley I spent some time listening to a Marsh Warbler singing, having never heard one in song before. For much of that time it mimicked a Song Thrush most convincingly, but occasionally it uttered some extremely rich, full-toned notes of its own varied and attractive song.

Instead of remaining in the valley, I went on down to Sandwich Bay; in retrospect, a wrong decision, for at Stodmarsh a Golden Oriole was heard singing, a Spoonbill and two Red-footed Falcons were also seen! When I returned there in the evening, having seen little of interest at Sandwich Bay, the weather had changed. A cold northerly wind was blowing strongly once again and heavy cloud hung from the sky. Such is one's luck in this fascinating, but at times most frustrating, pursuit.

By the end of May my total had reached 175 and might reasonably have exceeded 180. Early June produced a spate of rarities in the county, including two or three Caspian Terns and a Lesser Grey Shrike.

June 10th High time I added another rarity to *my* list! News of the shrike had reached me the previous evening and shortly after dawn I arrived at Seasalter and had the good fortune to study this most obliging bird at close range. It spent most of its time perched on telegraph wires, from which it occasionally hawked for insects in the dew-covered grass, returning to the wires before devouring its catch.

From here I went on to Thornden Wood, where I saw my first Redstart of the year, as it flew from its nest of six eggs in the roots of an upturned tree. In the same clump of conifers I also glimpsed five or six Crossbills, calling as they flew among the top-most branches.

June 15th A brief afternoon visit to Hingershall Park, Tunbridge Wells enabled me to add Wood Warbler. In a small area of mature birch trees and a scattering of young oaks there were at least two collecting food, but sadly I did not hear the beautiful song that so endears to me this attractive warbler, whose olive green upper parts contrast so vividly with the white belly. Its breeding distribution in Kent is now very thin and mainly confined to the western fringes of the county.

June 19th The numbers of Nightjars in Kent also appear to be on the decline, so I made a particular effort to visit various areas of chestnut coppice, their favoured habitat in this county. At Challock, despite the drizzly conditions, I heard the distinctive 'churring' shortly after 2100 hours. Though the light was bad I had some excellent close views of the wing clapping display flight and of the perched bird as it churred. In the same area two Woodcock were roding and as one flew immediately overhead I was able to hear the low croaking call, as well as the usual 'tsiwick' note.

June 28th One of the highlights of my year was the discovery of a Woodchat Shrike at my local study area. It stayed for five days, during which time I had excellent views of it, often perched on the hop wires from which it made frequent forays to catch insects.

July 6th While walking to school, I heard the clamour of several Blackbirds and Song Thrushes from the churchyard in East Sutton. I stopped and looked around, expecting to see a Little Owl or possibly a cat, but after a few seconds I caught sight of a young Tawny Owl on the ground by a gravestone. It allowed me to approach within a metre or two, its dark eyes not leaving me for a moment. When it eventually flew, the last downy feather drifted slowly to earth.

July 14th An unexpected phone call took me to Langley again to add yet another shrike species, this time a Red-backed Shrike. All four shrikes in Kent in one year must be a unique experience and, astonishingly, three were on my own study area! This individual was a rather elusive female, but she did provide me with some good views and it was interesting to watch two Willow Warblers behaving quite aggressively towards her. The next day she was joined by an attractive male. The Red-backed Shrike is another bird that this county has virtually lost as a breeding species.

July 27th A drake Red-crested Pochard in eclipse plumage was present in Mote Park, but it was probably not a genuine vagrant. Though they do occur in Britain in early autumn, the behaviour of this individual suggested that it was more likely to be an escaped bird.

July 31st An early morning visit to Sandwich Bay was most profitable. Several Whimbrel were feeding on the golf links and I was then fortunate enough to see the hen Montagu's Harrier that was summering there. This is quite a rare species in the county and I had not seen one in Kent before.

Just to show how fortuitous this pursuit can be we decided to visit North Foreland rather than Stodmarsh, as my companion had not yet seen Eider this year. Arriving there we bumped into a local bird-watcher, who told us that a Black Guillemot had been rescued from Broadstairs beach and taken to a local vet. A brief phone call, and a short while later I was able to study this charming species at close quarters. It seemed to be in good health and was devouring fish voraciously. It was released a few weeks later. The Black Guillemot is extremely rare in Kent and this was only the fourth record this century. In such circumstances I am not sure that it should 'count' on my annual list, but it still stands as a fascinating record.

August 1st I had received reports of a Black-necked Grebe at Bough Beech reservoir the previous evening, so the early morning found me once again in the west of the county and, with my present good fortune holding well, the bird was still present. It was an immature and dived frequently quite close to the shore. A duck Garganey was also present, showing an extremely well-marked face pattern and it was nice too to see two newly fledged Little Ringed Plover chicks.

August 2nd If you can find an area with the right conditions to attract migrant waders, watching them can be an absorbing pastime. Cliffe Pools often provides such a spot in early August and during a two hour period I identified fifteen different species in an area no more than fifty by one hundred metres. Most significant for the year's list was the presence of an adult Little Stint and twenty adult Curlew Sandpipers in varying stages of plumage, from the red of almost full summer to the grey of winter. There were nearly a hundred Dunlin and Ringed Plover, nine Ruff, four Grey Plover, one of them in almost full summer dress, two Greenshank and Whimbrel, single Little Ringed Plover and Spotted Redshank, again in almost full summer plumage.

August 13th Another visit to the same pool coincided with low tide and there were just three waders there! However, one of them was a Temminck's Stint, a regular but uncommon visitor to the county. In the poor evening light its white outer tail feathers flashed prominently as it flew.

Common Terns – feeding over the 'patch' at Dungeness

August 15th A steady trickle of passerine migrants was being reported from Dungeness and I saw my first Pied Flycatcher of the year there. A brief seawatch produced a flock of about twenty Black Terns on the 'patch', with at least ten Little Gulls and two or three Arctic Terns. An attractive pale phased adult Arctic Skua disturbed the feeding terns briefly.

I paid a rewarding visit to Boughton Park in the evening. As dusk fell the distinctive outline of a Hobby was silhouetted against the sky, as it attempted to take a Swallow. I then studied its plumage as it perched in a dead beech tree and identified it as a juvenile. A few minutes later three Barn Owls tumbled out of their nest hole and glided away to hunt for their evening meal. With a family of Kestrels and several Little Owls also present, it was a pleasing variety of birds of prey to see in such a short space of time.

Into the hundred and nineties now, with a good chance of seeing another twenty or so species, I felt confident of exceeding my target.

August 18th I made an early evening visit to Bewl Bridge reservoir with a vague hope of seeing an Osprey. Luck was with me. While scanning the woodland on the far shore I saw a large bird of prey perched on a dead pine. With my telescope I could make out sufficient detail to identify it as an Osprey. I watched patiently for an hour, hoping to see it in flight or possibly fishing, when it is quite magnificent, but it did not oblige.

August 20th With some easterly aspect in the wind a good variety of night migrants were appearing in the county, including good numbers of Icterine Warblers, Red-backed Shrikes and Wrynecks. I visited Dungeness and spent some time watching an Icterine Warbler in the moat round the Observatory. Although it is an almost annual autumn visitor to Kent, I had not seen one before.

During a seawatch, a White-winged Black Tern flew close to the 'patch'. It was an immature and provided me with good views, showing clearly the 'saddle' effect of the dark mantle and light wings.

August 21st I made another early morning visit to Bough Beech reservoir hoping to see the Red-necked Phalarope that had been reported. Although I searched hard and waited patiently for four hours, it had obviously continued its passage south and I had to be content with two Wood Sandpipers, five Ringed Plovers and a few Little Ringed Plovers and Common Sandpipers.

August 25th Strong S–SW winds brought heavy rain on the 24th and I felt such conditions might provide some interesting seabirds at Dungeness. Though I carried out a four-hour watch, I saw little, apart from very distant views of two large shearwaters, which I was unable to identify. Close to I saw two Arctic Skuas and about fifty Black Terns over the 'patch'.

Later in the day, however, I did add another rarity to my Kent list, when an immature Barred Warbler was trapped and ringed at the Observatory.

September 9th In early September the wind direction is again an important factor when deciding where to go and what species to look for. If you wish to watch seabirds, particularly skuas in the Thames Estuary, then a strongish wind in the northerly quarter is best. On this day the wind was NW 3–4 and I spent three and a half hours at Shellness. Although I saw a total of sixteen Arctic Skuas, the wind was not sufficiently strong to cause a big movement. However, as the tide dropped, exposing the mussel beds, there was an excellent opportunity to study at closequarters such waders as Oystercatcher, Turnstone, Curlew, Dunlin, and Grey and Ringed Plovers.

September 13th Back to Shellness again with a NE 4 wind blowing, but during a one and a half hour seawatch only one Arctic Skua was seen. However, I was delighted to have good views of a Manx Shearwater, which flew within two hundred metres of the shore.

September 14th One of the most exciting aspects of this hobby is finding and identifying a species for the first time. There is an added satisfaction when it is particularly rare.

But first, to keep this annual diary in order, I must describe the morning's events when I visited Langley again. I had heard reports of Siskins from several localities, surprisingly early, particularly after their absence the previous winter, and I was pleasantly surprised when I heard two calling as they flew over my head.

In the afternoon I visited Cliffe Pools at high tide, to check the wader roost and it was there that I had the good fortune to find a Buff-breasted Sandpiper, an American species. It was a most attractive small wader, so different in its habits and plumage. It spent much of its time hunting for insects amongst the clumps of glasswort, frequently stabbing its bill upwards.

I discovered later in the day that one had also been seen at Dungeness, just two hours earlier, and in fact the Cliffe bird had been found by others on the 10th! Nevertheless, it was a memorable day in my birdwatching calendar.

September 18th Strong NE winds produced a spate of seabird records along the east coast, with the largest numbers off Yorkshire and Norfolk, though several Great Skuas and two Sooty Shearwaters were seen off the Kent coast. The efficient 'grape vine' had also brought news of a putative Western Sandpiper at Pegwell Bay, but no amount of searching could locate it. However, I was blessed with my first ever

Sabine's Gull, an immature, and also an adult Mediterranean Gull in Pegwell Bay. In addition, during a two hour seawatch from Foreness Point, I was able to identify a Leach's Petrel, though there was no sign of any other seabird movement.

September 21st Following another phone call I arrived at Bough Beech reservoir shortly after dawn and managed to get sufficiently good views to identify an immature Spotted Sandpiper, which had been found there the previous day. It was, however, quite a challenge to separate it from the Common Sandpipers with which it could be compared. Its different structure and voice were as important as the minor plumage differences. With this species I achieved my target of 200.

This was proving to be an exceptional autumn for American waders in Kent, with the two Buff-breasted Sandpipers, two White-rumped Sandpipers, a Pectoral Sandpiper and now a Spotted Sandpiper, all in less than a month.

September 25th The conditions were ideal for a fall of migrants, with a SE wind and overnight showers as the front came through. Early this morning, while walking through the Observatory trapping area at Dungeness, many Lesser Whitethroats and Redstarts were flying from bush to bush, when I caught a glimpse of a larger warbler. It turned out to be an immature Barred Warbler. During the next hour I looked carefully at numerous small passerines and also had good views of a migrant Sparrowhawk. Suddenly a small robin-sized bird dived for cover under a bush – a Bluethroat? By calling other observers to surround the bush and sitting patiently for a while, we were eventually rewarded with excellent views of this attractive migrant, showing quite a lot of blue and chestnut on the breast. Walking back towards the Observatory I disturbed a Wryneck and later had the pleasure of studying one in the hand, as it was examined and ringed by the Observatory staff. The plumage detail is quite remarkable and its habit of twisting its neck is amazing to witness.

During a brief seawatch I had excellent close views of another immature Sabine's Gull, which had been present all week. A quite memorable day!

October 2nd After a week of SW winds the forecast indicated a swing to the NW. The wind blew quite strongly at Shellness, but failed to swing much north of W. Consequently there was little skua movement, though I did have excellent close views of two Great Skuas, my first for the year.

October 16th The Merlin is a regular autumn migrant and winter visitor to Kent, particularly on the coastal marshlands, but for me it seems to be quite a rarity. So I was extremely pleased to catch a glimpse of one at Dungeness and watch it chasing amongst Starling flocks as they came in to roost at the Oppen Pits.

In east Kent around this time there were reports of Lapland Buntings, a Shore Lark and a Tawny Pipit, with both Yellow-browed Warbler and Red-breasted Flycatcher at St. Margaret's Bay. Towards the end of the month single Bonelli's and Pallas's Warblers were trapped at Dungeness, but by the time I could visit there the weather had changed.

November 1st The last few days in October and the first week of November quite frequently produce interesting vagrants, but the wind direction is again critical. Sadly, it was still SW when I visited Sheppey and there was no likelihood of any seabird passage. I spent about four hours at Shellness while the tide came in and studied the waders as their feeding grounds became covered. The most interesting bird was a Purple Sandpiper, possibly the same individual back for its third winter at Shellness. It was nice, too, to see a Grey Plover still in breeding plumage. Large numbers of waders, including Dunlin, Grey Plover, Knot and Turnstone were flying to roost in the fields behind the Shellness hamlet.

November 5th An immature Long-tailed Skua, quite a rarity in Kent, had been present at Dungeness for nearly two weeks before I ventured south to see it. It was most obliging and displayed itself in splendid fashion, at times hovering over the sea a mere four or five metres away and paddling its feet in the brine. The well-marked, fine barring on the underwing and undertail coverts made it a most attractive bird.

Sea passage had been quite good in the early morning, with three Sooty Shearwaters before I arrived. I did manage to identify a Razorbill satisfactorily for the first time this year and several Gannets, Kittiwakes and Little Gulls could be seen. I also had good views of an immature Purple Sandpiper, which is quite unusual here, and excellent views of an adult Mediterranean Gull as it flew within fifty metres along the shoreline.

November 13th I spent six hours seawatching at Shellness. The force 4 wind eventually veered to the NW and there was some passage between mid-day and three o'clock. Kittiwakes were passing steadily in flocks of five to seventy and about 740 were counted. The other most numerous species were 205 Brent Geese and 115 Common Scoter. A total of fifteen Great Skuas and four divers, including two Red-throated, were satisfactorily identified, but the only addition for the year was a group of three Velvet Scoter flying into the Swale with a flock of Common Scoter.

November 15th An afternoon visit to Shellness again enabled me to locate a small flock of Lapland Buntings. I eventually had some excellent views, as they fed in a ploughed field behind the hamlet.

During the next ten days the wind blew strongly, first from the NW and then from the NE and a good variety of interesting species was seen in the Thames Estuary, with some marked movements of seabirds. Unfortunately, I was unable to visit either Shellness or Allhallows at this time, and missed such species as Little Auk, Puffin, Guillemot, Grey Phalarope, Buzzard, Whooper Swan and a late Pomarine Skua, all of which would have been additions to my year-list.

November 27th A four hour seawatch at Shellness failed to produce any new species, but I did see one Great Northern and fifteen Red-throated Divers, four Velvet Scoter and three Great Skuas, including one at rest on the beach. Maybe I should have gone to Dungeness, where over a hundred divers of all three species, large numbers of auks, including one Little Auk, and three Whooper Swans were identified during prolonged seawatches.

December 15th Reports of Avocets and Shore Larks at Sandwich Bay in recent weeks attracted me to that area. The tide was ideal, reaching high in the early afternoon. There was no sign of any Shore Larks along the beach or at the point. However, I did locate two Avocets feeding on the mud in Pegwell Bay. They eventually came to roost with the other waders, amongst which was a wintering Little Stint, on the shingle-covered point a short way from where I was patiently sitting.

December 30th At Cliffe Pools, while I was checking the area in preparation for another New Year's day trip, I was most fortunate to find a single Shore Lark, a pleasing addition with which to conclude a most successful year with a total of 210 species.

I stopped making regular visits to my local patch at Langley in 1982, which gave me more time to visit localities countywide. In that year I improved my annual total to 220, while in 1984 I was even more successful, reaching 230 on December 31st.

It is interesting to compare the progress during the three years by noting the totals reached at the end of selected months:

	Jan	Mar	May	Aug	Oct	Dec
1977	123	140	175	194	204	210
1982	138	143	195	207	216	220
1984	140	149	203	211	226	230

The 1984 total owes a lot to the efficient grape-vine that exists in Kent. In the autumn, I had a purple patch between September 30th and October 7th, when I saw the following species: Purple Heron, White-rumped Sandpiper, Long-billed Dowitcher, Rustic Bunting, Booted Warbler – the first Kent record – Yellow-browed Warbler and Red-breasted Flycatcher.

Birdwatching Calendar

The annual cycle of bird seasons, their breeding, wintering and migration behaviour, is a pattern we enjoy, knowing that essentially it is unchanging. We can look forward each spring to hearing the Willow Warbler sing and watching the Great Crested Grebe display. Field trips can be arranged, as necessary, to enjoy these and many other events year after year, though it is often the unexpected that adds that little bit extra to this absorbing hobby.

In this chapter I include a summary of expected events for each month. Then I list a selection of possible trips, which, over the year, should produce an interesting variety of birds in different habitats. Most of the localities mentioned warrant frequent visits throughout the year to gain the most from them, but that defeats the object of this chapter. You may, however, feel that some feature too frequently, while others do not feature enough. It will obviously depend on your own particular interests, they are merely suggestions based on my own experiences – the choice is yours.

Planning trips in advance can be fun and quite stimulating. I suggest that you consult the Systematic List, which gives you information on where and when each species is most likely to be seen. You should bear in mind that most coastal trips will be influenced by the state of the tide, while falls of migrants and seabird passage will be controlled by certain weather conditions. This means that a little flexibility in your planning will improve your chances of seeing particular species. Map references for the localities mentioned are included in Appendix II.

January

This is a month of relative stability, as far as birds are concerned. Certainly, in mild conditions, little change can be expected. Visits to the coastal marshes will produce wintering waders and wildfowl, while inland, in addition to our resident species, there are winter thrushes, like Fieldfare and Redwing; and finches such as Brambling and Siskin to be seen. But, when hard frosts persist, survival becomes the key-note, and birds will seek food wherever it is most available. Snow-storms and severe frosts locally may well restrict or prevent feeding, and initiate cold-weather movements. Severe weather conditions on the Continent may well cause an influx of rare grebes, like Red-necked and Slavonian; unusual geese, such as Barnacle or Bean; and diving duck, like Smew and Goosander, while northerly gales will bring seabirds, such as divers and auks that winter in the North Sea, closer to our shores, particularly around Thanet.

Elmley RSPB Reserve
Peregrine and Hen Harriers. Wildfowl and waders. White-fronted Goose flocks sometimes come to roost at dusk. Short-eared Owls – more often seen in late afternoon.

Sandwich Bay and Stonar Lake
Snow Buntings and Twite. Waders roosting at high tide. Check Stonar lake for diving duck and possibly rare grebes. Enquire at the Observatory.

Folkestone Harbour, Copt Point and the Warren
Gulls roosting in the harbour at high tide, with the Mediterranean at Copt Point – on the rocks, or feeding over the sewage outfall offshore. Purple Sandpipers roosting at high tide on the harbour walls, or on the concrete apron below the Warren. Fulmars prospecting along the cliffs. Black Redstart and Rock Pipit also feed around the apron.

Dungeness and Walland Marsh
Grebes and ducks on the pits, sometimes including Smew and Goosander. Look for Glaucous Gull by the fishing boats at the high tide gull roost, or on Lade Sands as the tide drops.

The Woolpack area attracts Bewick's Swans, with Hen Harriers roosting in the reedbed there at dusk. Golden Plover on the marsh often favour the Fairfield area.

Glaucous Gull – an adult roosting near the fishing boats at Dungeness.

February
A cold spell early in the month frequently produces increased numbers of wintering wildfowl, but as the month draws on it becomes less and less likely to produce much change. Warmer, sunny days will stimulate some species to sing, while the Grey Heron will return to the heronry to repair its nest, and possibly commence breeding.

Stodmarsh
In icy conditions, Bittern and Water Rails are sometimes more easily seen. Bearded Tits and Cetti's Warblers feed and call amongst the reeds. Siskins frequent the alders. If you are lucky, a Great Grey Shrike might perch atop hawthorns. Roosting Hen Harriers can be observed at dusk. Check the log entries in the information hut.

Shellness and Capel Fleet
Park near the hamlet and check the beach area for finches and buntings. Either side of high tide is best for watching the flocks of waders flying to and from their roosts – view from the point. Brent Geese feed in the fields as well as on the mud. Great Crested Grebes and possibly Red-throated Divers swim offshore.

Capel Fleet – scan from a high point initially to locate the White-fronted Goose flock. Golden Plover flock in the fields. Hen Harriers hunt widely. Walk to the Swale from Sayes Court for Twite on the saltmarsh and waders roosting at Harty – close to the Ferry House Inn. Short-eared Owls and possibly Barn Owl hunt towards dusk.

Bewl Bridge Reservoir and Bedgebury Pinetum
Wildfowl, grebes and possibly divers – best viewed from several points along the southern shore. There is a hide, too, overlooking the Nature Reserve.

Find a high point to scan the pinetum for a Sparrowhawk. Hawfinches and other finch species come to roost in the cypress trees towards dusk.

Northward Hill, Cooling Marshes and Cliffe Pools
The heronry is impressive late in the month. White-fronted Geese, Hen Harriers and Golden Plover occur on Cooling Marshes – view from the river wall or various footpaths. Grebes and ducks at Cliffe Pools, where the Ringed Plover roost at high tide is worth checking. Check Cliffe Quarry, too, for grebes and ducks.

March
A period of change commences about mid-month, when the earliest summer migrants, like Chiffchaff, Wheatear and Little Ringed Plover begin to arrive, and resident birds show signs of breeding behaviour. Wintering wildfowl and waders steadily disappear from the North Kent Marshes, with the last White-fronted Geese, for instance, usually leaving during the third week. The up-Channel passage commences with Brent Geese and Common Scoter.

Bough Beech Reservoir
Late wintering duck. First Little Ringed Plovers. View from the road across the north end.

New Hythe and River Medway
A good selection of flooded gravel pits on both sides of the railway. Walk around the various pits and along the river. Wintering grebes and ducks. Dunlin and Ruff occasionally feed on the river mud at low tide. Sand Martins and Little Ringed Plovers.

Dungeness
Early migrants and sea passage.

Sevenoaks Wildfowl Reserve
Ducks and migrant waders. A carefully managed gravel pit reserve with hides. Check visiting arrangements with the warden.

April
Traditionally a time of great change, when spring takes over from winter. In recent years, however, cold spells have frequently delayed not only the breeding behaviour of resident species, but the departure of winter visitors and the arrival of summer migrants. By mid-month, though, you can expect a considerable increase in the volume and variety of song as the Nightingales and warblers arrive. Each visit to any gravel pit, lake or park will produce something different at this time of year.

Pegwell Bay and Foreness Point
Essentially for waders. Watch from the shore between the hoverport and Stonelees as the tide rises in Pegwell Bay. Then visit Foreness Point, or the other small bays around the coast to Kingsgate, where Purple Sandpipers and other waders roost at high tide. Fulmars nest here and sometimes Eider are on the sea.

Elmley RSPB Reserve
Migrant waders and possibly Garganey.

Dungeness
For passerine migrants and sea passage. Sandwich Terns and possibly Garganey on the Reserve.

Sandwich Bay and Stodmarsh
Migrants generally – enquire at the Observatory. At Stodmarsh check the log entries in the information hut. If you remain until dusk, you may be rewarded with the calls of Spotted Crake or Bittern. The Snipe's display flight is worth seeing – and hearing.

May
A most exciting month. Large numbers of breeding summer visitors arrive, while some resident birds have fledged young. Species that breed within the Arctic circle stop off briefly to feed, or pass up-Channel. A warm southerly airflow brings with it a promise of rarities.

With such a variety of species in the county and many of them in song, it is a good opportunity to test your ear. Trying to unravel the complex sounds of the dawn chorus, though, can be bewildering until you have sorted out the songs of the resident species.

Fagg's Wood and Hamstreet Wood
The former is predominantly coniferous, with associated species like Goldcrest, Coal Tit and possibly Crossbill, but with clearings that attract Tree Pipits and warblers. The latter consists mainly of broad-leaved trees, with chestnut coppice. Excellent for Nightingales and woodland species, including Hawfinch. Park at south end of Saxon Shore Way.

Dungeness
The month for specialities like Pomarine Skua, during seabird movements, plus numerous passerine migrants. Study the terns on the 'patch' – but avoid high tide when they tend to roost.

Lyminge Forest
Predominantly coniferous, with Firecrests and Goldcrest, but also Tree Pipits, various warblers and possibly Sparrowhawk. Park in the public carpark just east of Six Mile Cottages.

Stodmarsh and Westbere
Savi's and Grasshopper Warblers, Bearded Tits feeding young. Possibly Hobby and Marsh Harrier, and such rarities as Purple Heron. The dawn chorus is quite special, with both woodland and marshland species, and may include a Bittern booming. Walk the length of the river, on the north bank, between Fordwich and Hersden lake.

June
A little less hectic than May, but still a great deal to be seen. It is the best time to study some of the breeding species that arrive late, like the Nightjar. A good month, too, for southern rarities.

Hungershall Park and Knole Park
Wood Warbler at the former, with Redstart, Tree Pipit and all three woodpeckers at the latter.

Church Wood RSPB Reserve
Tree Pipit, Redstart and Nightingale. Various walks are possible in this large woodland area, but the Reserve entrance is at the Rough Common end. Find a high view point to scan for raptors – on the road by Blean Wood possibly.

Dungeness RSPB Reserve
Breeding Roseate Terns and Mediterranean Gulls.

Challock Forest or Hurst Wood, Mereworth
Nightjars and Woodcock – evening visits required. Both most easily located by listening for their unique calls towards dusk.

July

The long period of autumn migration commences for Arctic breeding waders, and some of the adults can be seen in quite good plumage. It is still a busy time for breeding birds, some attending their second broods. A chance, too, to become familiar with the differences between the adult and immature plumages of various species that sometimes cause identification problems.

Bough Beech Reservoir
Little Ringed Plovers with young.

Stodmarsh
Various ducks and warblers will have fledged young. Hobbys may be hunting for food.

Elmley RSPB Reserve
Broods of ducks and geese. Returning migrant waders.

August

As the month progresses, increasing numbers of migrant visitors occur. Waders are flocking around the coast and on the coastal marshes. Winds from the east will tend to bring Scandinavian night migrants, like the Pied Flycatcher and the rarer Wryneck to our north and east facing shores, and occasionally inland. Frequent visits to various localities around the coast are tempting.

Yantlet Creek and Stoke Lagoon
Little Terns flock at the mouth of the creek, roosting on the shingle at high tide. Follow the creek south from its mouth for about three kilometres to find Stoke Lagoon on your right. Migrant waders and possibly Garganey.

Elmley RSPB Reserve or Cliffe Pools
Excellent for waders at this time of year, including Little Stints and Curlew Sandpipers, and possibly a rare, American sandpiper? Marsh Harriers, too, at Elmley, usually towards Windmill Creek.

Isle of Grain
The scrub between the village and the shore can be good for migrant passerines, when the wind is in the northeast. The Power Station outflow is excellent for studying terns, including Black and possibly the scarce White-winged Black Tern – best either side of high tide.

Shellness
Strong northerly winds late in the month will bring Arctic Skuas into the Thames and Swale. They can be seen well from the point, with the possibility of other seabirds too. Good numbers of shore waders can also be seen well on the mud here, either side of high tide.

September

During the month there is a subtle change in the mixture of migrants. This is the peak time for departing Swallows and House Martins, while Willow Warblers are slowly replaced by Chiffchaffs. By the end of the month summer migrants are becoming scarce and are being replaced by a more autumnal mixture of Robins, Goldcrests and Firecrests.

Seabird movements tend to include a greater variety of species, while wader flocks should be constantly checked for rarities. Scarce eastern and northern warblers, and other passerines may drift west and land around the coast, if the weather is right.

Dungeness Bird Observatory – one of the Heligoland traps in the moat surrounding the Observatory building.

Dungeness

Mainly for passerine migrants in the trapping area, but study the gulls and terns on the 'patch', where there will be immature and adult plumages to sort out. A strong south-easterly wind and showers may produce Sooty Shearwaters.

Allhallows, Shellness or Foreness Point

As in late August, strong northerly winds initiate seabird movements, which can be studied from all these vantage points. The Thames and Swale Estuaries usually attract larger numbers of skuas, with more shearwaters off Thanet.

Elmley RSPB Reserve
More migrant waders to sort out, many in fresh, juvenile plumages. The estuary feeders come in to roost at high tide – impressive numbers, too, on occasions.

St. Margaret's Bay
Passerine migrants, with rarer Scandinavian vagrants in the right weather. Park before you reach the lighthouse at the head of the valley, down and around which you can walk, following the various footpaths.

October

This is another very exciting month in the birdwatching calendar, marked by constant change. The last summer visitors leave and winter visitors start to arrive in large numbers. The passage of diurnal migrants, like Chaffinches and Starlings, can be most impressive around the coast. On the sea, northerly gales may produce rarer seabirds, like Leach's and Storm Petrels, or Sabine's Gulls, as well as Gannets, Manx Shearwaters, skuas, Common and Velvet Scoters, and Brent Geese. More fortunate, or regular, seawatchers may also see raptors such as Short-eared Owl, Sparrowhawk or even Rough-legged Buzzard coming in off the sea. Eastern rarities, like Pallas's and Yellow-browed Warblers can be anticipated when there is a predominantly easterly airflow.

Allhallows, Shellness or Foreness Point
Seawatching, when the conditions are right.

Dungeness
Visible migration of thrushes and finches. Falls of migrants may include Ring Ouzels, Black Redstarts and Firecrests. Seabird passage too – most obvious here in south-easterly winds.

Sandwich Bay or Thanet
A spell of easterly weather late in the month may well produce rare warblers amongst the Goldcrests, Firecrests and Chiffchaffs – to be found in any coastal scrub or copse.

November

The pattern for late October continues, but at a steadily decreasing rate early in the month, with winter thrushes now widespread and very few summer visitors remaining. Seabird movements have a more wintry mixture and may include flocks of Bewick's Swans and more Brent Geese, with divers, sea-duck like Eider and the rarer Long-tailed, and auks. November is the best month for Little Auks and Puffins. The numbers of wintering wildfowl and waders on the North Kent Marshes, and elsewhere, increase during the month.

Allhallows, Shellness or Foreness Point
Seawatching, when the conditions are right – that includes foul weather and gale force winds.

Hollingbourne to Harrietsham and Leeds Castle
This is one of many downland walks along the Pilgrim's Way where you might see a Sparrowhawk, or possibly a Buzzard. Partridges are easier to see at this time of year, while conifers will have Coal Tits and Goldcrests, and the beech-mast may attract Bramblings. The new lake at Leeds Castle can be approached from the Broomfield road and usually has a variety of wildfowl, plus Snipe and possibly Kingfisher.

The combination of two different habitats produces a good variety of species. Similar walks can be planned elsewhere along the Downs, near Westwell to include Eastwell Park, for example.

South Medway
Brent Geese, Red-breasted Mergansers and wintering grebes and waders. Either side of high tide is best to bring the birds close to the shoreline. Some vantage points are close to roads, while short walks will find others from which to view Funton Creek and Chetney Marshes; Ham Green and Half Acre; Rainham and Bartlett Creeks, from Motney Hill; and Copperhouse Marshes from Sharp's Green – the spit opposite Nor Marsh.

December
As in January, a severe spell of weather on the Continent can produce an influx of rarer grebes, geese and duck. But in milder conditions, such species as White-fronted Goose, Smew and Goosander may not arrive in any numbers until the New Year. Large flocks of Lapwings and Golden Plover are present on the coastal marshlands, and at various inland localities, while the rarer visitors, such as Great Grey Shrike, Shore Lark and Lapland Bunting may be much sought after, particularly if they have not been found earlier in the year!

Your choice of localities this month may well be influenced by what you missed the previous winter – though not everyone keeps annual lists.

Reculver to Minnis Bay and Chislet Marshes
Shore waders and duck. Hen Harriers over the marshes. A possible area for Shore Lark and Lapland Bunting.

Chislet Marshes can be viewed from Marshside, or a higher vantage point to locate any wintering geese or swans. Various footpaths divide the marshes.

New Hythe and River Medway
The largest pit, between the railway and the river, attracts wintering grebes and large numbers of duck. Cetti's Warblers are now resident here and at Burham Marsh, on the opposite side of the river, where Bearded Tits may winter.

The Leybourne lakes are also worth visiting, with a chance of Kingfisher.

South Swale Local Nature Reserve
Brent Geese and waders. Best either side of high tide when they feed on the mud close to shore. At high tide scan the mouth of the Swale for wintering flocks of Great Crested Grebes, Red-throated Divers and possibly a few Velvet Scoter.

Park near the Sportsman Inn and walk west along the seawall – a KTNC reserve. Hen Harrier and Short-eared Owl might be hunting over Graveney Marshes, while you might be lucky to find Snow Buntings and even a Shore Lark.

Systematic List

The systematic list follows the order and nomenclature of Dr. K.H. Voous, as published in *List of Recent Holarctic Bird Species* (1977). It includes all species satisfactorily identified in Kent from 1970–83. The names of the additional 28 species on the county list, recorded prior to this period, are included in Appendix I.

The bar charts, which show at a glance when a species is most likely to be seen, are based on an analysis of the records of the Kent Ornithological Society for 1970–82, a selection of which is published annually in the *Kent Bird Report*.

Where appropriate, I have tried to indicate where you are most likely to see particular species and I have also added a few personal comments regarding identification and behaviour, based on my own experience.

In the descriptions of the species' principal status, the following terms have quite specific meanings for the period 1970–83:

Very rare	1 – 10 records
Rare	11 – 25 records
Scarce	26 – 50 records

Key to Bar Charts

Each month is divided into four 7 or 8 day periods, and it is that period to which each symbol refers. To avoid creating a false impression regarding frequency, individuals making long stays, such as early or late migrants, or those overwintering, may only be shown in the arrival or departure week.

Symbols

Symbol	Meaning	Symbol	Meaning
⊡	once only	*	bred in only one year
⊟	less than annual	**	bred less than annually
⊟	annual	***	bred annually
⊟	peak numbers		

71

Red-throated Diver

Gavia stellata

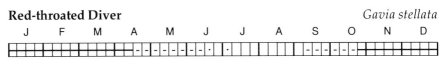

J   F   M   A   M   J   J   A   S   O   N   D

Winter visitor and passage migrant.

Favours sheltered localities in rough weather, but may be seen all round the coast and occasionally on inland waters. Flocks in the mouth of the Swale may occasionally exceed 100 in December–February, but day-totals rarely reach three figures off Dungeness, where the peak passage usually occurs in April.

Black-throated Diver

Gavia arctica

J   F   M   A   M   J   J   A   S   O   N   D

Occasional winter visitor and regular passage migrant.

May occasionally be seen on coastal and inland waters, but most regular on spring passage off Dungeness.

Great Northern Diver

Gavia immer

J   F   M   A   M   J   J   A   S   O   N   D

Passage migrant and occasional winter visitor.

The rarest of the three divers, being most regular on spring passage off Dungeness in late April and early May.
    In flight, compared with the other two divers, the feet appear to be strikingly large, but considerable experience is usually required before one can confidently separate these three species in flight. Even on the water they can provide problems (Sutherland, M.P. 1983)*.

*see The Field Identification of Divers in Winter Plumage, *Kent Bird Report* 30: 66–71.

Little Grebe
Tachybaptus ruficollis

| J | F | M | A | M | J | J | A | S | O | N | D |

Resident.   ★★★

Commonly seen on most inland waters, favouring small lakes and dykes for breeding. Large flocks may be seen in autumn and winter, with peaks of up to 300 at Cliffe Pools.

Great Crested Grebe
Podiceps cristatus

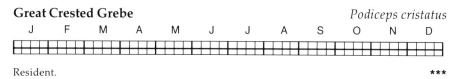

| J | F | M | A | M | J | J | A | S | O | N | D |

Resident.   ★★★

Breeds on the larger inland waters and gravel pits. Forms flocks around the coast in winter, which occasionally exceed 100, the favoured localities being Dungeness to Greatstone, Thanet, the mouth of the Swale and the south Medway.

Red-necked Grebe
Podiceps grisegena

| J | F | M | A | M | J | J | A | S | O | N | D |

Annual winter visitor and passage migrant.

May be seen around the coast and on inland waters, but in recent years most regular on the Dungeness gravel pits.

Slavonian Grebe
Podiceps auritus

| J | F | M | A | M | J | J | A | S | O | N | D |

Annual winter visitor and passage migrant.

Usually alone, but two or three are sometimes seen together around the coast and on inland waters.
   Beware of confusion with the next species, particularly when in intermediate plumages. In flight, note the extent of white on the wings. On the water look at the shape of the head and bill, and very carefully note the pattern of plumage on the head and neck.

Black-necked Grebe
Podiceps nigricollis

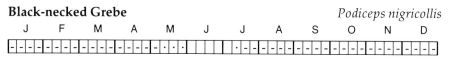

| J | F | M | A | M | J | J | A | S | O | N | D |

Annual winter visitor and early autumn passage migrant.

Usually seen in ones and twos, but occasionally four or five occur together in early autumn, favouring reservoirs and gravel pits.

Black-browed Albatross *Diomedea melanophris*

Very rare vagrant.

One off Foreness Point in December 1978 is the only county record.

Fulmar *Fulmaris glacialis*

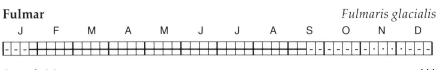

J	F	M	A	M	J	J	A	S	O	N	D

Annual visitor. ★★★

Nests on the cliffs between Thanet and Dover. Breeding birds now return to the nest sites in late December and depart by early September. May also be seen in the Thames Estuary and elsewhere around the coast.

Cory's Shearwater *Calonectris diomedea*

J	F	M	A	M	J	J	A	S	O	N	D

Very rare vagrant.

A possible reward for regular sea-watchers at Foreness Point or Dungeness.
    Beware the possibility of confusion with distant, juvenile Gannets.

Sooty Shearwater *Puffinus griseus*

J	F	M	A	M	J	J	A	S	O	N	D

Almost annual passage migrant.

The best opportunities occur in inclement weather conditions, particularly in northerly gales, from good sea-watching points like Foreness Point and Shellness.
    Beware confusion with the browner, Balearic race of the Manx Shearwater.

Manx Shearwater *Puffinus puffinus*

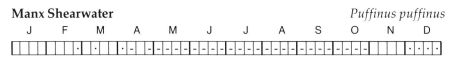

J	F	M	A	M	J	J	A	S	O	N	D

Annual passage migrant.

Best seen from suitable sea-watching vantage points in the Thames estuary, around Thanet and at Dungeness, where small flocks can occasionally be seen during the summer months. About one in five have been of the Balearic race *P.p.mauretanicus*.

Storm Petrel
Hydrobates pelagicus

| J | F | M | A | M | J | J | A | S | O | N | D |

Rare straggler.

Usually associated with northerly gales. Be at Foreness Point, in the mouth of the Swale, or at Allhallows.

Leach's Petrel
Oceanodroma leucorhoa

| J | F | M | A | M | J | J | A | S | O | N | D |

Rare straggler.

As with the Storm Petrel, usually associated with northerly gales.

Good views are required to separate these two petrels satisfactorily. Note the manner of flight, as well as plumage detail, most carefully. The rump and tail shape are difficult to see at a distance.

Gannet
Sula bassana

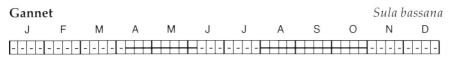

| J | F | M | A | M | J | J | A | S | O | N | D |

Passage migrant.

May be seen all round the coast, but peak day-totals, exceeding 100, are usually recorded in late autumn in the Thames Estuary, off Thanet or Dungeness.

Cormorant
Phalacrocorax carbo

| J | F | M | A | M | J | J | A | S | O | N | D |

Non breeding resident.

May be seen all the year round, though relatively few are present during May–July. Roosting flocks frequently exceed 50 and they occur regularly on some inland waters, like Leybourne and Bough Beech.

Shag
Phalacrocorax aristotelis

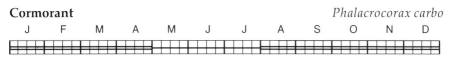

| J | F | M | A | M | J | J | A | S | O | N | D |

Recorded annually.

Relatively scarce, but most likely to be seen around Thanet.

Bittern
Botaurus stellaris

J   F   M   A   M   J   J   A   S   O   N   D

Resident and winter visitor.   ★★

Most regular in the Stour Valley, 'booming' in April–May. In severe winters, Bitterns may turn up anywhere in localities with reed-fringed, open water.

Little Bittern
Ixobrychus minutus

J   F   M   A   M   J   J   A   S   O   N   D

Very rare vagrant.

Only seven records, four of which have been in the Stour Valley.

Night Heron
Nycticorax nycticorax

J   F   M   A   M   J   J   A   S   O   N   D

Very rare vagrant.

Only eight records, in widely scattered localities.

Squacco Heron
Ardeola ralloides

Very rare vagrant.

One, present on the Thames marshes in July 1979, was the first county record this century.

Little Egret
Egretta garzetta

J   F   M   A   M   J   J   A   S   O   N   D

Rare visitor.

Early autumn birds may remain for several weeks on the North Kent Marshes.

Great White Egret
Egretta alba

Very rare vagrant.

The only county record concerns one, first seen in the Stour Valley and later at St. Margaret's, in May 1977.

Grey Heron *Ardea cinerea*

J	F	M	A	M	J	J	A	S	O	N	D

Resident.   ★★★

Up to nine heronries are usually occupied in the county, including the largest in Britain, at Northward Hill, with over 200 pairs.

It is an impressive sight, best viewed from within the Reserve, but it can be seen well, before the trees are in full leaf, from the road leading to Swigshole Cottage.

Purple Heron *Ardea purpurea*

J	F	M	A	M	J	J	A	S	O	N	D

Annual passage migrant.

Visit the Stour Valley in May and you may be lucky – though I haven't been, yet!

Black Stork *Ciconia nigra*

Very rare vagrant.

Singles at Littlebourne in May 1982 and on Thanet and Sheppey in June 1983.

White Stork *Ciconia ciconia*

J	F	M	A	M	J	J	A	S	O	N	D

Rare passage migrant.

More than half the records occurred during two spring influxes in 1976 and 1977, mainly in east Kent.

Glossy Ibis *Plegadis falcinellus*

Very rare vagrant.

One at Swanscombe in April–May 1974. One at Stodmarsh from December 1975 was joined by another in October 1979. They are still present in 1985, spending the winter at Stodmarsh and the summer on Sheppey.

Spoonbill
Platalea leucorodia

J	F	M	A	M	J	J	A	S	O	N	D

Scarce annual visitor.

Seen, usually in ones and twos, most frequently on coastal marshes, though larger parties occur occasionally. The bar chart excludes the records of one wintering in 1973/74 and one to three summering in 1974.

Visit Elmley during June–August.

Mute Swan
Cygnus olor

J	F	M	A	M	J	J	A	S	O	N	D

Widespread resident.　　　　　★★★

Non-breeding flocks may exceed 100 in the Stour Valley. Similar sized flocks may occasionally gather in the winter months on other, wet, lowland areas.

Bewick's Swan
Cygnus columbianus

J	F	M	A	M	J	J	A	S	O	N	D

Annual winter visitor and passage migrant.

Most regular on the Walland Marsh, near the Woolpack, where flocks of 100 or more may be seen. Smaller numbers winter intermittently on Sheppey, the Thames marshes, the Wantsum marshes, or in the Stour Valley.

Whooper Swan
Cygnus cygnus

J	F	M	A	M	J	J	A	S	O	N	D

Scarce winter straggler.

A few records of one to three occur in most winters, usually in association with the previous species.

Try to compare size with other swans and note the bill pattern very accurately.

Bean Goose
Anser fabalis

J F M A M J J A S O N D

Rare winter visitor.

Most likely to be seen on the Thames or Sheppey marshes, but becoming more regular and occurring in the Stour Valley and on Dengemarsh.
Note size, plumage detail and bare-part colours with great care. The two races show considerable variation.

Pink-footed Goose
Anser brachyrhynchus

J F M A M J J A S O N D

Scarce, but annual winter visitor or passage migrant.

Groups of one to six may occur occasionally on the North Kent Marshes or in the Stour Valley. Small flocks occur rarely, as in the severe winter of 1979.
Feral individuals may occasionally be seen in widespread localities, sometimes out of season.

White-fronted Goose
Anser albifrons

J F M A M J J A S O N D

Regular winter visitor.

The two main wintering areas are the Thames and Sheppey marshes, each supporting between 500–1,000 in most winters. The peak numbers may not occur until February.
On Sheppey, find a high spot to view from – Capel Hill or Mocketts on Harty Hill. On the Thames, Cooling Marshes can be viewed from the river wall.

Greylag Goose
Anser anser

J F M A M J J A S O N D

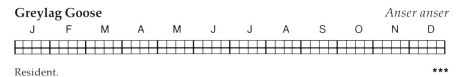

Resident. ***

Feral populations are thriving on the Thames, Medway and Sheppey, in the Stour Valley, at Dungeness and inland at Sevenoaks. Occasionally, immigrants from the east, with pink bills, may be seen in winter on Sheppey, or at Sandwich Bay.

Snow Goose

Anser caerulescens

Very rare vagrant.

Most records of this species are likely to refer to escapes. However, a flock of 17 on the Thames in March 1980 certainly included one genuine vagrant from Canada (see *Kent Bird Report* No. 29). Another flock of seven was present on Elmley in January–February 1982.

Canada Goose

Branta canadensis

J	F	M	A	M	J	J	A	S	O	N	D

Resident. ★★★

A highly successful, introduced species, now breeding throughout the county. Flocks of 500 or more may be seen at Sevenoaks, Bough Beech and Bewl Bridge in the autumn.

Barnacle Goose

Branta leucopsis

J	F	M	A	M	J	J	A	S	O	N	D

Scarce winter visitor.

Genuine migrants are most likely to occur with the wintering grey geese, or occasionally with Brent Geese. Exceptional influxes occurred in February 1979 and 1981.

Confusion with feral birds is inevitable, as free-flying birds are bred at one or two localities in the county.

Brent Goose

Branta bernicla

J	F	M	A	M	J	J	A	S	O	N	D

Winter visitor and passage migrant.

One or two birds have summered. Wintering flocks can be seen regularly in the south Medway and in the Swale. In late March and April, up-Channel passage is quite marked off Dungeness, while in late October and early November a marked passage can be seen off Thanet and in the Thames Estuary, particularly in northerly winds.

Birds of the pale-bellied race *B.b.horta* occur rarely.

Red-breasted Goose

Branta ruficollis

Very rare vagrant.

The only county record concerns one in the Stour Valley in October 1978.

Egyptian Goose   *Alopochen aegyptiacus*

Resident.

A feral species, which may occasionally be seen in the Stour Valley and elsewhere.

Ruddy Shelduck   *Tadorna ferruginea*

Possible vagrant.

A rare visitor, whose origins must usually remain in doubt. This species is kept in captivity and feral populations occur on the Continent.

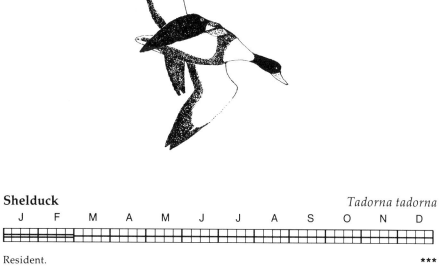

Shelduck   *Tadorna tadorna*

J	F	M	A	M	J	J	A	S	O	N	D

Resident.   ★★★

The three estuaries in north Kent may each attract 1,000–3,000 birds in winter. Post-breeding creches may total 300 at Cliffe Pools. Also common inland at Bough Beech, where several pairs now breed.

Mandarin

Aix galericulata

Resident.

Small, feral populations are widely scattered, but most often seen in central and west Kent. Try the river Len near Leeds Castle.

Wigeon

Anas penelope

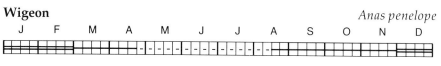

Winter visitor. ★★

Between 5,000–10,000 may be seen in each of the three north Kent estuaries during December–February, with over 20,000 occasionally at Elmley. Far smaller numbers occur elsewhere around the coast, with some wintering on Bewl Bridge and Bough Beech Reservoirs. A few sometimes remain throughout the summer months and single pairs occasionally breed.

American Wigeon

Anas americana

Very rare vagrant.

The three records have all occurred during April–May, the two most recent on Elmley in 1982 and 1983.

Gadwall

Anas strepera

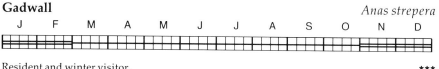

Resident and winter visitor. ★★★

Winter flocks in excess of 50 occur regularly in the Stour Valley, on Sheppey and the Thames marshes, but Gadwall can be seen occasionally on most inland waters and coastal marshes, where they still favour freshwater.

Teal

Anas crecca

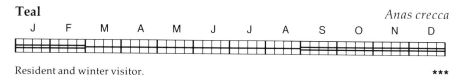

Resident and winter visitor. ★★★

Widespread during the winter months, with peak numbers occasionally reaching 5,000 in the Medway Estuary. A few pairs breed on the North Kent Marshes and in the Stour Valley.

Individuals of the North American race, the Green-winged Teal *A.c.carolinensis*, were present in November 1981 and April–May 1983, the latter at Elmley.

Mallard
Anas platyrhynchos

J	F	M	A	M	J	J	A	S	O	N	D

Widespread resident. ★★★

Early autumn and winter peaks frequently exceed 1,000 on the Dungeness Reserve, on Walland Marsh, in the Stour Valley and in the three estuaries of north Kent.

Pintail
Anas acuta

J	F	M	A	M	J	J	A	S	O	N	D

Winter visitor. ★★

Up to 500 may be present in the Medway Estuary during the winter months, with far fewer in the other estuaries. Occasionally occurs on inland waters. A few sometimes remain throughout the summer months and single pairs occasionally breed.

Visit Funton Creek on the south Medway, or Elmley for good views of this most elegant duck.

Garganey
Anas querquedula

J	F	M	A	M	J	J	A	S	O	N	D

Summer visitor. ★★

Breeding usually confined to the North Kent Marshes and the Stour Valley. Although fairly widespread on passage, including inland waters, relatively few birds are involved. Autumn flocks only rarely exceed 20.

Blue-winged Teal
Anas discors

Very rare vagrant.

The first county records concern singles present in the Stour Valley in April 1970 and May–June 1978.

Shoveler
Anas clypeata

J	F	M	A	M	J	J	A	S	O	N	D

Resident and winter visitor. ★★★

Breeds on freshwater marshes. The highest winter concentrations of 400 or more usually occur on Elmley, but common on all coastal marshes. Small numbers also visit inland waters.

Red-crested Pochard *Netta rufina*

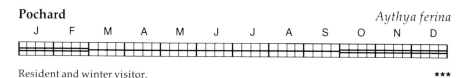

Scarce visitor.

The situation is confused by the presence of escaped birds, but mid-summer and autumn records probably include some genuine vagrants from the Continent.

Pochard *Aythya ferina*

J F M A M J J A S O N D

Resident and winter visitor. ★★★

Breeds quite commonly on the North Kent Marshes and in the Stour Valley. Winter concentrations occasionally exceed 500 on Dungeness Reserve, Cliffe Pools and inland at New Hythe and Bewl Bridge Reservoir. Small numbers may also be seen on most inland waters.

Ring-necked Duck *Aythya collaris*

Very rare winter visitor.

There are six or seven records, all of single drakes, with the first county record at Stodmarsh in April 1972, followed by others at Westbere in February, and Sevenoaks in April and November 1977, at Dungeness in December–January 1979/80, November 1980 and again in January 1981.

Ferruginous Duck *Aythya nyroca*

J F M A M J J A S O N D

Rare vagrant.

There are several records, mainly in recent years, but the situation is not only confused by possible escapes, but also by 'aythya' hybrids. It is essential to make detailed field notes at the time, noting in particular the bill colour, including the extent of black on the 'nail' if possible.

Tufted Duck *Aythya fuligula*

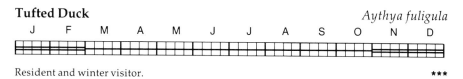

Resident and winter visitor. ★★★

Winter flocks occasionally exceed 500 at Cliffe Pools, with smaller numbers widespread on all inland waters. Breeding also occurs in widespread localities, including small ponds.

Scaup

Aythya marila

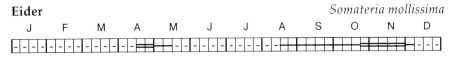

Winter visitor.

Occasionally seen in mid-summer. May be seen on passage around the coast, but shows a preference for freshwater pits and lakes. Has become quite scarce in recent years.
Try the lakes at Murston.

Eider

Somateria mollissima

J	F	M	A	M	J	J	A	S	O	N	D

Regular visitor and passage migrant.

Essentially a sea duck. Small flocks of non-breeding birds may favour one locality throughout the year and can usually be seen along the north coast between the Swale and Thanet, or off Dungeness, where small numbers are also recorded on both spring and autumn passage. Late autumn passage off Thanet may also be quite marked.

Long-tailed Duck

Clangula hyemalis

J	F	M	A	M	J	J	A	S	O	N	D

Winter visitor and passage migrant.

Occasionally one to two may winter on freshwater pits close to the coast, like those at Cliffe, Stonar or Dungeness. Exceptionally, wintering individuals may remain into the summer. On passage, records are almost annual off Dungeness in spring and in the Thames Estuary in autumn.

Common Scoter

Melanitta nigra

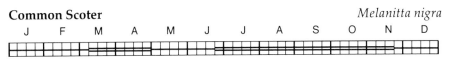

Passage migrant.

A marked spring passage up-Channel may be witnessed off Dungeness between late March and early May, where day totals sometimes exceed 5,000. Smaller numbers are seen on autumn passage all around the coast, and small flocks may be seen at anytime of the year. Overland passage is confirmed by annual records at Bough Beech Reservoir.

Velvet Scoter

Melanitta fusca

J F M A M J J A S O N D

Passage migrant.

Essentially a coastal species. Spring passage off Dungeness in late April and early May may rarely produce day totals of 200 or more. In late autumn, small numbers occur regularly in the Thames Estuary.

Visit Shellness or Allhallows during periods of seabird passage in strong northerly winds in late autumn.

Goldeneye

Bucephala clangula

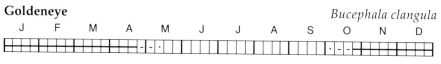

J F M A M J J A S O N D

Winter visitor.

Flocks in excess of 50 may occasionally be seen in the south Medway, from Motney Hill, but smaller numbers regularly winter on inland waters and gravel pits countywide. Singles summered in 1975 and 1980.

Look for the drakes displaying during March at Dungeness.

Smew

Mergus albellus

J F M A M J J A S O N D

Regular winter visitor.

Small numbers are most frequently seen on the gravel pits in the Dungeness area, but in severe winters Smew may occur on any sizeable inland waters remaining open. Over 100 were present in the severe winter of 1979.

The magnificent drake is relatively rare, but the ducks, in their own way, are also most attractive.

Red-breasted Merganser

Mergus serrator

J F M A M J J A S O N D

Winter visitor and passage migrant.

Small flocks winter regularly in the Swale and in the Medway Estuary. Off Dungeness this species features regularly on up-Channel spring passage in small numbers. Rare on inland waters.

Goosander
Mergus merganser

J	F	M	A	M	J	J	A	S	O	N	D

Winter visitor.

Recorded more frequently than Smew, but only in small numbers. The pits at Dungeness and the reservoirs and gravel pits in west Kent are favoured. It is relatively scarce in north Kent. Over 130 were present in the severe weather of February 1979.

Ruddy Duck
Oxyura jamaicensis

J	F	M	A	M	J	J	A	S	O	N	D

Winter visitor.

Since the first county record at Bough Beech in November 1970, this species has become a regular visitor, with most records from Bough Beech and Dungeness. Summering at Bough Beech in 1983 may point to breeding soon.

  An attractive, welcome addition to the county list.

Honey Buzzard
Pernis apivorus

J	F	M	A	M	J	J	A	S	O	N	D

Scarce passage migrant.

There were only eleven records during 1970–78, but four, four, ten and eight during the next four years. Is it possible that breeding might be confirmed soon?

Black Kite
Milvus migrans

J	F	M	A	M	J	J	A	S	O	N	D

Rare vagrant.

The first county record concerns one over Luddesdown in May 1976, followed by two to three annually from 1980–83.

Red Kite
Milvus milvus

J	F	M	A	M	J	J	A	S	O	N	D

Scarce vagrant.

Sightings are now annual and increasing, with nine, five, six and seven during 1979–82.

Marsh Harrier
Circus aeruginosus

J	F	M	A	M	J	J	A	S	O	N	D

Summer visitor and passage migrant.   *

An annual visitor, increasing in numbers. Most regular on spring and autumn passage, with Sheppey and the Stour Valley offering the best opportunities for observing this fine raptor. Now summering more regularly, a pair bred successfully in 1983. Singles have also over-wintered.

Hen Harrier
Circus cyaneus

J	F	M	A	M	J	J	A	S	O	N	D

Winter visitor.

Over 40 may now winter, a marked increase noted since the severe winter of 1979, when over 100 were present. Most regular on the North Kent Marshes, in the Stour Valley and on Walland Marsh.

Check Stodmarsh, or the reedbed near the Woolpack on Walland Marsh, where up to ten birds roost fairly regularly.

Montagu's Harrier
Circus pygargus

J	F	M	A	M	J	J	A	S	O	N	D

Passage migrant.

Much rarer than the other two harriers, though almost annual in the Sandwich Bay area and on Sheppey. Some individuals occasionally make prolonged stays.

Goshawk
Accipiter gentilis

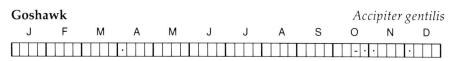

J	F	M	A	M	J	J	A	S	O	N	D

Very rare straggler.

Scandinavian migrants are indicated by the autumn records at Reculver, Sandwich Bay and St. Margaret's, but falconers' birds do escape from time to time.

Sparrowhawk

Accipiter nisus

| J | F | M | A | M | J | J | A | S | O | N | D |

Resident, winter visitor and passage migrant. ★★

Still relatively scarce, though numbers are increasing. Coastal migrants can be seen regularly in late October.

Buzzard

Buteo buteo

| J | F | M | A | M | J | J | A | S | O | N | D |

Annual visitor and passage migrant.

Occurrences have increased to 10 or more a year and a few have wintered regularly since 1979, while summer records suggest that breeding may yet be proven.
    A good description is important to eliminate other Buzzard species.

Rough-legged Buzzard

Buteo lagopus

| J | F | M | A | M | J | J | A | S | O | N | D |

Irregular winter visitor and passage migrant.

Most regular as a passage migrant in late October. Occasional influxes occur, as in 1973/74 and 1974/75, while a few individuals may be present in other winters. Sheppey and the Wantsum marshes are the favoured areas.

Osprey

Pandion haliaetus

| J | F | M | A | M | J | J | A | S | O | N | D |

Annual passage migrant.

On average, ten birds occur per year. Autumn visitors occasionally make more prolonged stays. The Stour Valley and reservoirs in west Kent attract Ospreys almost annually.

Kestrel
Falco tinnunculus

J	F	M	A	M	J	J	A	S	O	N	D

Resident.

Autumn numbers are supplemented by migrants. The motorway verges provide good hunting grounds for this attractive falcon, which hovers while searching for prey.

Red-footed Falcon
Falco vespertinus

J	F	M	A	M	J	J	A	S	O	N	D

Rare spring vagrant.

Eight of the sixteen records have occurred at the county's two Observatories, four staying for periods of seven to fifteen days.

Merlin
Falco columbarius

J	F	M	A	M	J	J	A	S	O	N	D

Winter visitor.

Up to ten winter regularly, with three or more in the Dungeness area, in the Stour Valley and the North Kent Marshes, but they may not be easy to find.

Try scanning the fields at Leysdown, where the waders come in to roost; you may see one perched on the ground.

Hobby
Falco subbuteo

J	F	M	A	M	J	J	A	S	O	N	D

Summer visitor and passage migrant.   ★★

Numbers vary from year to year, but one or two wooded sites may be visited annually and breeding is becoming more regular.

To observe this species hunting Sand Martins or Swifts is a magnificent spectacle and Stodmarsh or Bough Beech might provide that opportunity.

Gyrfalcon
Falco rusticolus

Very rare vagrant.

One at Folkestone in April 1979 is the only county record.

Peregrine
Falco peregrinus

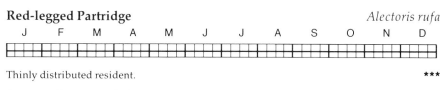

Winter visitor and passage migrant.

A relatively scarce species, with only two to five records annually between 1970–78, but now wintering regularly. Can we hope that this striking species will return to breed?
   Visit the Elmley Reserve in mid-winter to see this magnificent falcon.

Red-legged Partridge
Alectoris rufa

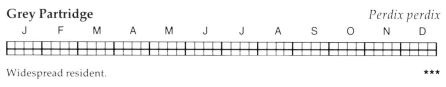

Thinly distributed resident.   ★★★

Scarce on Sheppey and Thanet, but common on the Thames marshes.
   Artificial stocking in some areas may involve the closely related Chukar *A.chukar*.

Grey Partridge
Perdix perdix

Widespread resident.   ★★★

In winter, several family parties often form into large coveys.

Quail
Coturnix coturnix

Scarce summer visitor.   ★

Occasional 'Quail years' may produce over 20 reports, as in 1970, but less than 10 is more usual. An extremely elusive species, so sight records are rare.
   Listen for the distinctive 'wet-my-lips' call-note from cereal crops, particularly towards dusk.

Pheasant
Phasianus colchicus

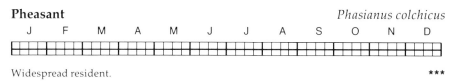

Widespread resident.   ★★★

The population is artificially stocked by shooting interests.

Water Rail
Rallus aquaticus

J	F	M	A	M	J	J	A	S	O	N	D

Resident and winter visitor. ★★★

Widespread during the winter months, but generally limited to the Stour Valley and the North Kent Marshes during the breeding season.

Another species whose presence is more easily established by hearing its various calls, or its attractive song, which involves a trilling sound.

Spotted Crake
Porzana porzana

J	F	M	A	M	J	J	A	S	O	N	D

Rare visitor.

One to three records almost annually, with 70% along the Stour Valley between Westbere and Sandwich Bay.

Listen for the 'whip' call-note at Stodmarsh in late April.

Corncrake
Crex crex

J	F	M	A	M	J	J	A	S	O	N	D

Rare passage migrant.

Only exceptionally good fortune will produce a Kent record of this species.

Moorhen
Gallinula chloropus

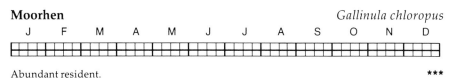

Abundant resident. ★★★

Extremely widespread, found on even the smallest of ponds.

Coot
Fulica atra

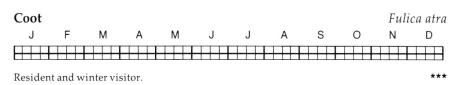

Resident and winter visitor. ★★★

Widespread, with large flocks occurring in the winter months, occasionally exceeding 1,000 at Cliffe, Westbere, Dungeness, Bough Beech and Bewl Bridge.

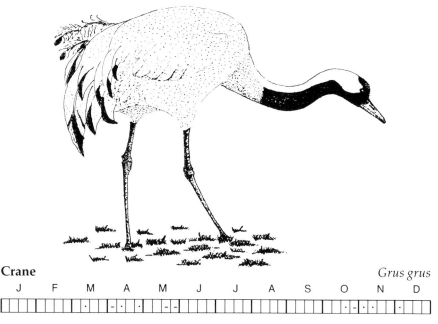

Crane

Grus grus

J	F	M	A	M	J	J	A	S	O	N	D

Rare vagrant.

There were no records during 1970–76, but there have been annual sightings since. In October–November 1982, there was an exceptional influx involving over 100 birds, following which one overwintered on Chislet Marsh.

Great Bustard

Otis tarda

Very rare vagrant.

The only county records this century concern two at St. Margaret's in January 1970, one on Chislet Marsh from January–April 1978, and three and one respectively on Walland and the Thames marshes in December 1981.

Oystercatcher

Haematopus ostralegus

J	F	M	A	M	J	J	A	S	O	N	D

Resident and winter visitor. ★★★

The largest breeding population is on the Medway Islands. A flock of up to 3,000 winters regularly in the Swale, with smaller numbers all round the coast. Passage migrants are occasionally seen at inland reservoirs and gravel pits.

Be at Shellness before high tide, to witness an impressive spectacle, as they fly in to roost, either on the point or at Harty.

Black-winged Stilt
Himantopus himantopus

Very rare vagrant.

Singles were present at Dungeness in June–July 1978, on Sheppey from June–August 1980 and in May 1981, and at Yantlet Creek in September 1982.

Avocet
Recurvirostra avosetta

J	F	M	A	M	J	J	A	S	O	N	D

Passage migrant.   *

Most regular on spring passage at Dungeness or Sandwich Bay, when flocks of 10–20 may sometimes be seen. Flocks of 74 and 70 on Dungeness Reserve in June 1980 and December 1982 respectively were quite exceptional. A few occasionally winter now on the North Kent Marshes, while summer records are also on the increase, with one pair breeding successfully in 1983.

Cliffe Pools and Elmley probably offer the best opportunities to see this rather special wader.

Stone Curlew
Burhinus oedicnemus

J	F	M	A	M	J	J	A	S	O	N	D

Rare vagrant.

Since successful breeding ceased at Dungeness in 1965, this species has become an increasingly rare visitor, with one to three records less than annually.

Collared Pratincole
Glareola pratincola

Very rare vagrant.

The first county records concern singles at Sandwich Bay during September–October 1976 and at nearby Pegwell Bay in November 1977.

Little Ringed Plover
Charadrius dubius

J	F	M	A	M	J	J	A	S	O	N	D

Summer visitor and passage migrant.   ***

A dozen or more pairs breed annually, mostly in west Kent. Most easily seen at Bough Beech Reservoir, but small numbers pass through the county from late July, when they can be seen regularly at other sites, like Cliffe Pools and Dungeness Reserve. One was present at Sevenoaks during December–January 1977/78.

Ringed Plover
Charadrius hiaticula

J	F	M	A	M	J	J	A	S	O	N	D

Passage migrant, winter visitor and summer resident.　　　★★★

Flocks of 500 or more occur in most years during August, at Cliffe Pools, in the Medway and Swale, and at Sandwich Bay. Smaller numbers are present all around the coast, with occasional records inland. This species has recently commenced breeding at several inland sites.

Kentish Plover
Charadrius alexandrinus

J	F	M	A	M	J	J	A	S	O	N	D

Passage migrant and occasional summer visitor.

Occurring more regularly in recent years, with up to 40 in 1980. Most often seen at Sandwich Bay and Dungeness, particularly on the ARC Pit, but in several recent winters there has been one at Cliffe Pools, roosting with the Ringed Plovers.

Confusion with juvenile Ringed Plovers is possible, though, as is quite often the case in bird identification, if you have any doubt, then it probably isn't! They are, simply, very different in size, shape and plumage.

Dotterel
Charadrius morinellus

J	F	M	A	M	J	J	A	S	O	N	D

Scarce passage migrant.

Most records concern one to five birds, usually at various coastal localities, including Sandwich Bay in four recent springs. Flocks of 12–13 occurred in May 1973 and 1974.

Regular checks of exposed, flat fields, along the Downs or Manston Airport, for example, might prove worthwhile during May.

Lesser Golden Plover
Pluvialis dominica

Very rare vagrant.

The first county records concern singles at Grove Ferry in April–May and again at nearby Westbere in June 1978, with another at Elmley in May 1982.

Golden Plover   *Pluvialis apricaria*

J	F	M	A	M	J	J	A	S	O	N	D

Winter visitor and passage migrant.

Flocks, totalling several thousand birds, may be seen during the winter months, on the pasture lands of the Thames marshes and Sheppey, the marshes between Sandwich and Herne Bay, and on Walland Marsh. One or two inland localities south of Ashford and Sutton Valence regularly attract smaller numbers, but this species is rare in the west of the county.

Most attractive are the birds of the northern race *P.a.altifrons* that can be seen in breeding plumage, while on passage in late spring.

Grey Plover   *Pluvialis squatarola*

J	F	M	A	M	J	J	A	S	O	N	D

Winter visitor and passage migrant.

Favours estuarine mudflats and may be seen all round the coast, but is rare inland. Each of the three estuaries in north Kent may occasionally hold over 1,000 birds in the winter months.

Look for this species in its fine breeding plumage, particularly in May. Visit the Elmley Reserve at high tide, where they roost.

Sociable Plover   *Chettusia gregaria*

Very rare vagrant.

One seen at Headcorn in December 1979 is only the third county record.

Lapwing   *Vanellus vanellus*

J	F	M	A	M	J	J	A	S	O	N	D

Resident, winter visitor and passage migrant.   ***

A widespread species throughout the county, forming large flocks in the winter months. From early June post-breeding flocks may be seen flying westerly, while severe weather conditions in winter can cause quite spectacular southerly movements.

If it was less common, I am sure that this most attractive wader would be appreciated far more.

Knot
Calidris canutus

J	F	M	A	M	J	J	A	S	O	N	D

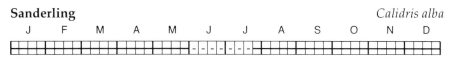

Winter visitor and passage migrant.

An estuarine species, rarely seen inland. Most numerous in the Swale, where several thousands may be present in the winter months.

Watch the Shellness roost for a magnificent spectacle. In late spring you may be fortunate enough to see some in their beautiful 'red' breeding plumage.

Sanderling
Calidris alba

J	F	M	A	M	J	J	A	S	O	N	D

Winter visitor and passage migrant.

Relatively unusual in north Kent and rare inland, this species favours the sandy flats at Lade, Sandwich Bay and around Thanet. The largest numbers often occur during peak migration in March and October.

Though unmistakable as it runs along the shore, following the ebb and flow of the sea, individuals do cause some identification problems, either by feeding atypically, like a Dunlin, or in breeding plumage, when they resemble the much smaller Temminck's Stint.

Little Stint
Calidris minuta

J	F	M	A	M	J	J	A	S	O	N	D

Regular passage migrant.

Favours the muddy fringes of freshwater marshes, but may be seen at inland reservoirs and gravel pits. Occasionally occurs on estuarine mud.

Cliffe Pools and Elmley will usually produce this species in August–September, but remember, only the autumn juveniles have the distinctive double 'V' on the mantle and scapular feathers.

Temminck's Stint
Calidris temminckii

J	F	M	A	M	J	J	A	S	O	N	D

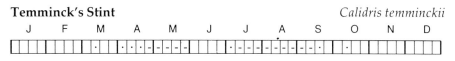

Passage migrant.

There are six records per year, on average, most often of single birds. Favours freshwater localities, usually around the coast, but occasionally seen inland.

Showing white sides to the breast, it may resemble a small Common Sandpiper at a glance.

Least Sandpiper
Calidris minutilla

Very rare vagrant.

The only county record concerns one near Sandwich in October 1976.

White-rumped Sandpiper
Calidris fuscicollis

Very rare vagrant.

Between 1977–81 there were nine autumn records during August–October. There are only two earlier Kent records.

Baird's Sandpiper
Calidris bairdii

Very rare vagrant.

One at Bough Beech in September 1973 is only the second county record.

Pectoral Sandpiper
Calidris melanotos

J	F	M	A	M	J	J	A	S	O	N	D

Rare vagrant.

Most frequently recorded in the Dungeness area, but seen almost annually at Elmley since 1978.

Curlew Sandpiper
Calidris ferruginea

J	F	M	A	M	J	J	A	S	O	N	D

Regular passage migrant.

Essentially a freshwater wader favouring muddy pools around the coastal marshes, though it will feed on the muddy foreshore. As with Little Stints, the autumn passage of adults precedes that of the immatures.

Get to know its call, its more elegant, long-legged 'jizz' and check for its white rump to avoid possible confusion with the long-billed, northern race of the Dunlin.

Purple Sandpiper
Calidris maritima

J	F	M	A	M	J	J	A	S	O	N	D

Winter visitor.

Between 70–100 winter regularly on Thanet and can best be seen when roosting at high tide in Margate Harbour, or in the sheltered bays between Foreness and Whiteness. At other times scan the rocky foreshore. Smaller numbers winter near Folkestone and Dover, but elsewhere in the county it is relatively scarce.

Dunlin
Calidris alpina

J	F	M	A	M	J	J	A	S	O	N	D

Winter visitor and passage migrant.

A common wader all around the coast which is also frequently seen at inland reservoirs and gravel pits. About 40,000 probably winter in the three north Kent estuaries. A few non-breeding birds may remain throughout June.

Broad-billed Sandpiper
Limicola falcinellus

Very rare vagrant.

The first Kent record concerns one trapped and ringed at Harty in August 1970. Since then there have been singles at Cliffe in May 1982 and at Sandwich Bay in June 1983.

Buff-breasted Sandpiper
Tryngites subruficollis

Very rare vagrant.

In 1977 there were singles at Cliffe and Dungeness in September, with one at Elmley in October 1979 and another at Bough Beech in October 1981. There is only one earlier county record.

Ruff
Philomachus pugnax

J	F	M	A	M	J	J	A	S	O	N	D

Regular passage migrant and winter visitor. ★★

The first indication of successful breeding this century was recorded in 1981 and 1982. A bird essentially of freshwater marshes, it may be seen regularly at various localities like Cliffe Pools and Elmley, in the Stour Valley, or on the Dungeness Reserve. Flocks of 100–200 now winter.

Individual males in fine breeding plumage are worth looking for at Elmley in May–June.

Jack Snipe
Lymnocryptes minimus

J	F	M	A	M	J	J	A	S	O	N	D

Winter visitor and passage migrant.

A species that seems to favour the same marshy tracts year after year and these may be found throughout the county. Small flocks may occasionally winter together, but it is more usual to flush just one or two birds – provided that you practically tread on them!

It is a rare treat to study the beautifully marked plumage of one on the ground.

Snipe
Gallinago gallinago

J	F	M	A	M	J	J	A	S	O	N	D

Resident and winter visitor. ★★★

A widespread species in the winter months, to be found in most freshwater habitats. Flocks of 100 or more occur regularly in favoured localities, inland as well as around the coast.
   In the breeding season the curious drumming display can be witnessed at Stodmarsh.

Great Snipe
Gallinago media

Very rare vagrant.

Singles were seen at Sevenoaks in September 1975 and at Westbere in April 1978.

Long-billed Dowitcher
Limnodromus scolopaceus

Very rare vagrant.

One present at Elmley in July 1981 is only the second county record. Dowitchers, not specifically identified, were also seen at Harty in September 1970 and at Sandwich Bay in October 1973.

Woodcock
Scolopax rusticola

J	F	M	A	M	J	J	A	S	O	N	D

Resident and winter visitor. ★★★

In October–November migrants may be seen at coastal sites. Usually found in ones and twos in various types of woodland, but inevitably one has to practically tread on them before they rise. In the breeding season, coppiced areas are favoured and evening visits in May–June are a must to witness the curious 'roding' – display flights.

Black-tailed Godwit
Limosa limosa

J	F	M	A	M	J	J	A	S	O	N	D

Passage migrant and occasional summer visitor. ★★

May be seen all the year round at various localities on the North Kent Marshes. Large flocks build up in March–April and again from July–September, either in the Medway, or in the Swale. Only small numbers may be seen elsewhere.
   Another species that can be seen well on the Elmley Reserve.

Bar-tailed Godwit *Limosa lapponica*

J	F	M	A	M	J	J	A	S	O	N	D

Winter visitor and passage migrant.

The largest numbers winter in the Swale, where 400–500 may be present, but smaller numbers can be seen all round the coast. A marked up-Channel passage can also be observed off Dungeness in late April, while small flocks occasionally migrate overland.

Whimbrel *Numenius phaeopus*

J	F	M	A	M	J	J	A	S	O	N	D

Passage migrant.

A bird essentially of the coastal marshes, where roosting flocks of 50 or more may be seen in early May, or from late July–August. The up-Channel passage off Dungeness has peaked in the second week of May in recent years.

Listen for the distinctive call-note, a trilling whinny, from migrants flying high over the county during August, but beware of identifying this species in spring only by a distant call – the Skylark is an excellent mimic!

Curlew *Numenius arquata*

J	F	M	A	M	J	J	A	S	O	N	D

Winter visitor and passage migrant.

Flocks of over 1,000 may be seen in the Swale, or in the Medway during the winter months, or at times of peak passage from late July–September. Smaller numbers can be seen all around the coast, often feeding on the mudflats at low tide. Most inland records concern birds flying over.

Spotted Redshank *Tringa erythropus*

J	F	M	A	M	J	J	A	S	O	N	D

Passage migrant.

North Kent provides the most favoured freshwater, marshland habitat and there are comparatively few records from elsewhere in the county, though this species may occasionally be seen at inland localities.

In autumn, roosts of up to 100 or more occur in the Medway and on Elmley.

An early May visit to Elmley should provide the memorable sight of this species in its fine, dusky, breeding plumage.

Redshank

Tringa totanus

J	F	M	A	M	J	J	A	S	O	N	D

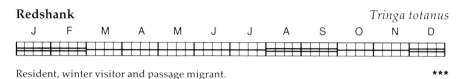

Resident, winter visitor and passage migrant.   ★★★

Very common all round the coast and on adjacent marshes, with small numbers occurring inland in suitably damp localities.

Marsh Sandpiper

Tringa stagnatilis

Very rare vagrant.

Singles were present at Cliffe in September 1979 and Elmley in May 1981 and August 1983.

Greenshank

Tringa nebularia

J	F	M	A	M	J	J	A	S	O	N	D

Passage migrant.

Tidal creeks and coastal freshwater marshes are favoured. The Medway, Swale and Stour estuaries attract the largest flocks in autumn, when up to 100 or more may gather to roost. Like the Spotted Redshank, it is wintering in small numbers with increasing regularity. The clear, triple call-note can sometimes be heard from overland migrants.

Greater Yellowlegs — *Tringa melanoleuca*

Very rare vagrant.

One seen in the Medway in November 1972 is only the second county record.

Lesser Yellowlegs — *Tringa flavipes*

Very rare vagrant.

In 1970 singles were present on Chetney in September and on Walland Marsh in October, with others on Elmley in September 1981 and again on Walland Marsh in April 1983.

Green Sandpiper — *Tringa ochropus*

J	F	M	A	M	J	J	A	S	O	N	D

Passage migrant and winter visitor.

Ones and twos may occur at any wetland habitat, even small ponds and streams throughout the county, with scattered groups of up to 30 during July–August at favoured sites like Sandwich Bay and Elmley.

Get to know the diagnostic, loud call-note, which has a Swallow-like quality, and observe the very dark wings and mantle, in flight, that contrast markedly with the white rump.

Wood Sandpiper — *Tringa glareola*

J	F	M	A	M	J	J	A	S	O	N	D

Passage migrant.

A relatively scarce migrant, particularly in spring, favouring coastal freshwater marshes and gravel pits, occasionally visiting inland reservoirs. Usually seen in ones and twos, but up to 15 may sometimes gather in August at localities like Elmley or Sandwich Bay.

With its longer legs, it is a more elegant wader than the previous species. Its whistling 'chiff-iff-iff' call-note is also diagnostic.

Terek Sandpiper — *Xenus cinereus*

Very rare vagrant.

The only county records concern singles at Sandwich Bay in May 1973 and Dungeness in August 1982.

Common Sandpiper
Actitis hypoleucos

J	F	M	A	M	J	J	A	S	O	N	D

Passage migrant.

Favours the muddy fringes of streams, ponds and larger areas of water countywide. In July–August scattered groups of 100 or more may be seen at Sandwich Bay, with smaller gatherings elsewhere. Ones and twos may remain throughout the winter months, most regularly in the Sandwich Bay area again.

Spotted Sandpiper
Actitis macularia

Very rare vagrant.

The only county records this century concern singles at Dungeness in May 1971 and Bough Beech in September 1977.

Turnstone
Arenaria interpres

J	F	M	A	M	J	J	A	S	O	N	D

Winter visitor and passage migrant.

Although present all round the Kent coast, this species has a preference for rocky shores. The largest flocks of around 500 may be seen at the high-tide roosts around Thanet during January–March. Similar numbers occasionally occur on autumn passage in the Swale.

In summer plumage this wader too is most attractive and well worth looking for.

Wilson's Phalarope
Phalaropus tricolor

Very rare vagrant.

The only county records concern singles seen on Walland Marsh in September 1970 and Egypt Bay in May 1971, with two at Dungeness in August 1979.

Red-necked Phalarope
Phalaropus lobatus

J	F	M	A	M	J	J	A	S	O	N	D

Rare passage migrant.

Ten of the fifteen records occurred during 1981–82, with four each at Elmley and Dungeness, three at Sandwich Bay and four elsewhere, all involving singles.

Its fine, delicate structure and unique feeding behaviour – spinning as it swims – make this one of my favourite wader species.

Grey Phalarope — *Phalaropus fulicarius*

J F M A M J J A S O N D

Scarce passage migrant.

Its occurrence is frequently associated with stormy weather. Apart from two singles inland at Bough Beech, the rest have been around the coast, often sheltering on waters behind the sea wall.

Pomarine Skua — *Stercorarius pomarinus*

J F M A M J J A S O N D

Passage migrant.

A short, but now annual, spring passage is observed off Dungeness in May, when small flocks may be seen flying up-Channel. In autumn, with strong winds in the northerly quarter, a few can be expected in the Thames Estuary.

Be at Dungeness in early May – in fine weather with southeasterly winds, or watch in autumn from Foreness, Allhallows or Shellness, where they sometimes gather in the mouth of the Swale.

Arctic Skua — *Stercorarius parasiticus*

J F M A M J J A S O N D

Passage migrant.

Spring passage off Dungeness may produce day-totals of up to 25, but the largest numbers are most likely to occur in the Thames Estuary, during northerly gales in autumn, when over 100 may be counted in a day.

Look for one chasing the terns over the 'patch' at Dungeness, or flying into the Swale in autumn.

Long-tailed Skua — *Stercorarius longicaudus*

J F M A M J J A S O N D

Rare passage migrant.

Almost annual since 1976, off Dungeness in the spring, or in the Thames Estuary in the autumn.

Great Skua
Stercorarius skua

J	F	M	A	M	J	J	A	S	O	N	D

Passage migrant.

Off Dungeness the spring passage is relatively light, but the autumn passage is more prolonged, with day totals in double figures. However, the Thames Estuary offers the best opportunities in autumn. In northerly winds they tend to gather in small flocks in the mouth of the Swale, before circling high and continuing their migration, possibly overland. Peak movements have involved over 100 birds in a day.

Be at Shellness, or on the south side of the Swale to witness these movements.

Mediterranean Gull
Larus melanocephalus

J	F	M	A	M	J	J	A	S	O	N	D

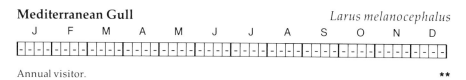

Annual visitor. **★★**

Essentially a coastal species, becoming increasingly regular and now breeding on the Dungeness Reserve. A small number now winter at Copt Point, Folkestone.

Get to know the immature plumages and check the gull flocks all round the coast – and at rubbish tips.

Little Gull
Larus minutus

J	F	M	A	M	J	J	A	S	O	N	D

Passage migrant.

Essentially a coastal species, but occasionally recorded on inland waters. The most marked passage occurs off Dungeness, where a few occasionally summer. Fairly regular too off Shellness and Thanet in the autumn.

A most attractive, small gull, with distinctive, black underwings in adult plumage.

Sabine's Gull
Larus sabini

J	F	M	A	M	J	J	A	S	O	N	D

Scarce passage migrant.

Most often seen off Dungeness – where individuals occasionally make prolonged stays – around Thanet and in the Thames Estuary, particularly in northerly winds in late autumn.

Another attractive gull, but beware possible confusion with immature Kittiwakes, when seen at a distance.

Black-headed Gull
Larus ridibundus

J	F	M	A	M	J	J	A	S	O	N	D

Resident and winter visitor. ★★★

There are large breeding colonies on the North Kent Marshes, particularly on the Medway Islands and in the Swale, with smaller numbers at Dungeness. Extremely widespread in the winter months, when flights to and from roosts at dawn and dusk are part of the everyday scene.

Slender-billed Gull
Larus genei

Very rare vagrant.

The only county record concerns one off Dungeness between July–September 1971.

Common Gull
Larus canus

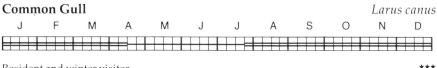

J	F	M	A	M	J	J	A	S	O	N	D

Resident and winter visitor. ★★★

A widespread species in the winter months, though less common than the Black-headed Gull well inland. A few pairs breed at Dungeness.

Lesser Black-backed Gull
Larus fuscus

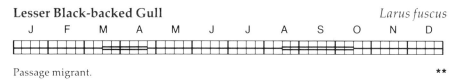

J	F	M	A	M	J	J	A	S	O	N	D

Passage migrant. ★★

A few pairs breed occasionally at Dungeness, or on the Dover cliffs. Often frequents rubbish tips, like the other gulls, and passage birds fly overland. The darker backed Scandinavian race *L.F.fuscus* is often the commoner species around the coast.

Herring Gull
Larus argentatus

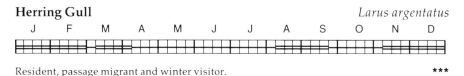

J	F	M	A	M	J	J	A	S	O	N	D

Resident, passage migrant and winter visitor. ★★★

Breeds commonly on the east Kent cliffs and at Dungeness, and increasingly on inland roof tops. Large numbers are attracted to rubbish tips. Birds of the yellow-legged race *L.a.michahellis* occur occasionally, mostly in autumn.

Iceland Gull
Larus glaucoides

J	F	M	A	M	J	J	A	S	O	N	D

Rare visitor.

Essentially coastal, becoming annual since 1979, with the first over-wintering record occurring in 1980/81.

Glaucous Gull
Larus hyperboreus

J	F	M	A	M	J	J	A	S	O	N	D

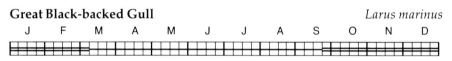

Annual visitor.

Wintering with increasing regularity at Dungeness and Sandwich, while singles have twice remained throughout the year at the former site.

Most easily seen at roost, with the other large gulls, by the fishing boats at Dungeness, but check your local rubbish tips for a glimpse of this huge 'owl-like' gull.

Great Black-backed Gull
Larus marinus

J	F	M	A	M	J	J	A	S	O	N	D

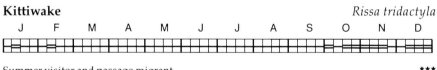

Winter visitor.

Essentially a coastal species, though attracted to inland rubbish tips too. Non-breeding birds remain throughout the summer.

Kittiwake
Rissa tridactyla

J	F	M	A	M	J	J	A	S	O	N	D

Summer visitor and passage migrant. ★★★

A pelagic species, though a few are seen inland annually. About 2,000 pairs now breed on the Dover cliffs and a regular post-breeding flock may be seen on the shingle at Dungeness in August. In autumn, north-westerly gales may produce large movements in the Thames Estuary, while in recent winters there have been a few huge movements off Thanet.

Gull-billed Tern
Gelochelidon nilotica

J	F	M	A	M	J	J	A	S	O	N	D

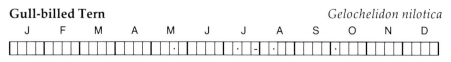

Very rare vagrant.

Only six records, all of coastal migrants.

Caspian Tern
Sterna caspia

J	F	M	A	M	J	J	A	S	O	N	D

Very rare vagrant.

Just eight coastal records, with one, more inland, at Stodmarsh.

Royal Tern
Sterna maxima

Very rare vagrant.

One present on Dungeness Reserve in June 1982 is only the second Kent record.

Sandwich Tern
Sterna sandvicensis

J	F	M	A	M	J	J	A	S	O	N	D

Summer visitor and passage migrant.   ★★

Has bred regularly on Dungeness Reserve since 1978. Recorded all round the coast, but relatively rare on inland waters. In spring there is a marked up-Channel passage off Dungeness, with day-totals of several hundreds.

Roseate Tern
Sterna dougallii

J	F	M	A	M	J	J	A	S	O	N	D

Summer visitor and passage migrant.   ★★

Has bred regularly on Dungeness Reserve since 1976, but it is scarce elsewhere around the coast.

Visit the 'patch' at Dungeness to watch this graceful tern fishing. Note the whiteness of the upperparts of the adults and the absence of black on their primary tips.

Common Tern
Sterna hirundo

J	F	M	A	M	J	J	A	S	O	N	D

Summer visitor and passage migrant.   ★★★

The 'sea' tern most likely to occur on inland waters. In spring a marked up-Channel passage occurs off Dungeness, with peak day-totals in the thousands. The largest breeding colonies also occur at Dungeness, with several smaller colonies on the North Kent Marshes.

Arctic Tern
Sterna paradisaea

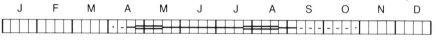

Passage migrant.

Marked movements may be witnessed off Dungeness. Regular too in the Thames Estuary in the late autumn. Only occasionally seen inland.

Study the terns over the 'patch' at Dungeness, or at the Isle of Grain power station outflow. Look for the translucent secondary and primary feathers in spring and note the distinctive, white secondary triangle on the upperwing of the immatures in autumn.

Little Tern
Sterna albifrons

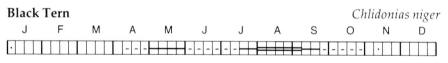

Summer visitor and passage migrant.   ★★★

Spring passage off Dungeness occasionally involves day-totals of up to 200 birds. Small numbers breed at several colonies on shingle around the coast, but the success rate is invariably poor, due in part to human disturbance. In autumn the peak numbers involve post-breeding flocks of 200–300 birds, usually at Shellness or Yantlet Creek.

Whiskered Tern
Chlidonias hybridus

Very rare vagrant.

The only county records concern singles, inland at Bough Beech in June 1973 and at Dungeness in late May and early June 1976.

Black Tern
Chlidonias niger

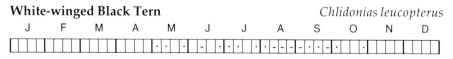

Passage migrant.

A marsh tern, which often favours inland waters, though the peak numbers, sometimes involving several hundreds, invariably occur offshore at Dungeness.

Visit the power station outflows at Dungeness or the Isle of Grain, particularly in autumn, to get good views of this most attractive tern.

White-winged Black Tern
Chlidonias leucopterus

Scarce passage migrant.

Ones and twos are almost annual at Dungeness, but rare elsewhere in the county.

Study the terns over the 'patch' in late August, looking for the dark mantle and contrasting pale wings of the immature bird.

Guillemot/Razorbill
Uria aalge/Alca torda

J	F	M	A	M	J	J	A	S	O	N	D

Annual winter visitors and passage migrants.

The offshore movements of the large auks inevitably restrict specific identification, though both species can be seen on the sea, close to the shore on occasions, particularly in the winter months. In recent years the Guillemot seems to have been more common.

Since 1979/80, winter seawatching has produced unprecedented day-totals of several thousand auks off Thanet. Often associated with strong northerly winds, there appears to be some link too with shoals of sprats. Northerly gales in autumn also bring auks into the Thames Estuary and they can be observed well off Warden Point or Allhallows. There is also a down-Channel passage, visible off Dungeness in the spring, and a corresponding up-Channel passage in the autumn.

Black Guillemot
Cepphus grylle

Very rare vagrant.

One off Deal in March 1972 and another off Thanet, which was rescued and later released in July 1977, are the only recent records.

Little Auk
Alle alle

J	F	M	A	M	J	J	A	S	O	N	D

Scarce autumn vagrant.

An oceanic species, but one to three records occur almost annually, most often during severe northerly gales. Occasionally, larger numbers may be driven south, as in October 1974, when over 40 were seen.

Try Allhallows, Shellness or Foreness Point in suitable conditions.

Puffin

Fratercula arctica

J	F	M	A	M	J	J	A	S	O	N	D

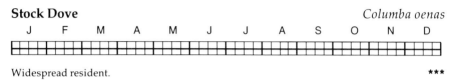

Annual passage migrant.

Only one to ten records occur annually, but Puffins may be expected during northerly gales in late autumn, in the Thames Estuary or off Thanet. Regular seawatching at Dungeness may produce occasional sightings.

   A difficult species to add to your Kent list, as it is usually seen in flight some way out to sea and only rarely actually swimming close to shore. Regular seawatching experience is essential to enable you to separate this species from the larger auks satisfactorily.

Stock Dove

Columba oenas

J	F	M	A	M	J	J	A	S	O	N	D

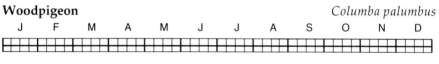

Widespread resident.   ★★★

A woodland species frequently seen in parkland and on open farmland. During the winter months, flocks of several hundreds may be seen on the drained marshes of north and east Kent.

Woodpigeon

Columba palumbus

J	F	M	A	M	J	J	A	S	O	N	D

Abundant resident and passage migrant.   ★★★

Large flocks form during the winter months and in severe weather southwesterly movements may be observed.

Collared Dove

Streptopelia decaocto

J	F	M	A	M	J	J	A	S	O	N	D

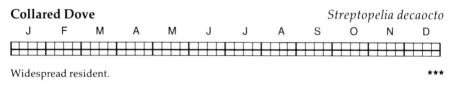

Widespread resident.   ★★★

Flocks. of up to 300 or more may be attracted to grain stores.

Turtle Dove

Streptopelia turtur

J	F	M	A	M	J	J	A	S	O	N	D

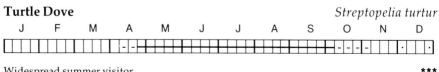

Widespread summer visitor.   ★★★

Visible migration in spring, involving several hundred birds in a day, may be witnessed at coastal localities, while autumn flocks may build up to 100 or more in early September.

   The attractive, gentle, purring song is a welcome breath of spring each year.

Ring-necked Parakeet
Psittacula krameri

J	F	M	A	M	J	J	A	S	O	N	D

Local resident. **★★**

Breeding regularly since the early seventies, the main population is still based on Thanet. Visit Northdown Park for a noisy reception from this attractive native of Africa and India.

Great Spotted Cuckoo
Clamator glandarius

Very rare vagrant.

One at Dungeness in August 1970 is the only county record.

Cuckoo
Cuculus canorus

J	F	M	A	M	J	J	A	S	O	N	D

Common summer visitor. **★★★**

Widespread as a breeding species, using a variety of hosts. The adults usually depart by early July, with peak numbers of migrants at Dungeness invariably during the third week, when up to 30 are sometimes present.

Barn Owl
Tyto alba

J	F	M	A	M	J	J	A	S	O	N	D

Resident. **★★★**

Thinly distributed throughout the county. Most obvious when hunting towards dusk. Visit Sheppey late on a winter's afternoon.

Scops Owl
Otus scops

Very rare vagrant.

One near Wye in October 1971 is only the second county record and the first this century.

Little Owl
Athene noctua

J	F	M	A	M	J	J	A	S	O	N	D

Widespread resident. **★★★**

The most widespread owl species in Kent, favouring agricultural countryside, but by no means restricted to it.

Often seen by day perched in the open, but in woodland the persistent calls of mobbing passerines may well locate one for you.

Tawny Owl
Strix aluco

| J | F | M | A | M | J | J | A | S | O | N | D |

Resident. ★★★

Favours mature woodland, but may frequently be heard calling in suburban districts and parkland, particularly towards dawn and at dusk.

Long-eared Owl
Asio otus

| J | F | M | A | M | J | J | A | S | O | N | D |

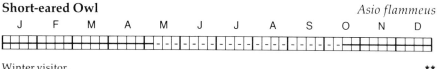

Uncommon resident and winter visitor. ★★★

Thinly distributed and difficult to locate, due to its nocturnal habits. It roosts in small flocks during the winter months and, once established, the same roost site may be used year after year.

Listen for its call at dusk or towards dawn in February from copses, with a few conifers, along the Downs.

Short-eared Owl
Asio flammeus

| J | F | M | A | M | J | J | A | S | O | N | D |

Winter visitor. ★★

A few pairs bred regularly until 1978. Favours the coastal marshes around the county, but comparatively rare inland. In late autumn it is fascinating to watch migrants arriving off the sea at Foreness Point or Shellness, while in winter groups of up to ten can sometimes be seen hunting together.

Visit Elmley or Harty on a winter's afternoon.

Nightjar
Caprimulgus europaeus

| J | F | M | A | M | J | J | A | S | O | N | D |

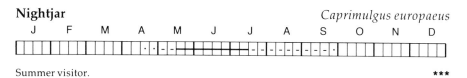

Summer visitor. ★★★

Possibly on the decline, the Nightjar favours chestnut coppice areas and young conifer plantations.

Towards dusk in June, listen for the distinctive 'churring' and then watch for the display flight, it is a memorable spectacle.

Swift

Apus apus

J	F	M	A	M	J	J	A	S	O	N	D

Abundant summer visitor. ★★★

Spectacular gatherings associated with thundery weather may occasionally be witnessed, when insects become concentrated in localised air currents.

Pallid Swift

Apus pallidus

Very rare vagrant.

One at Stodmarsh in May 1978 was the first record of this species to be accepted for the British Isles.

Alpine Swift

Apus melba

J	F	M	A	M	J	J	A	S	O	N	D

Very rare vagrant.

The nine records have all involved single birds, eight along the coast between Dungeness and Thanet and one inland at Haysden. Four were present for periods of two to five days.

Kingfisher

Alcedo atthis

J	F	M	A	M	J	J	A	S	O	N	D

Resident. ★★★

Quite widespread along the major river valleys and their tributaries. The dispersal of young birds in autumn produces a few coastal records, some remaining to winter.

Listen for the piercing call to locate this delightful bird.

Bee-eater

Merops apiaster

J	F	M	A	M	J	J	A	S	O	N	D

Very rare vagrant.

Seven coastal records, all of single birds, between Dungeness and Thanet, with another at Iwade.

Roller

Coracias garrulus

Very rare vagrant.

One near Dover in September 1980.

Hoopoe

Upupa epops

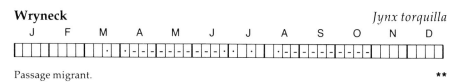

J	F	M	A	M	J	J	A	S	O	N	D

Annual passage migrant.

An average of six per year are recorded from widespread localities.
Try Dungeness in April–May.

Wryneck

Jynx torquilla

J	F	M	A	M	J	J	A	S	O	N	D

Passage migrant.   ★★

Sadly, breeding has not been confirmed since 1973. To see this fascinating bird in autumn, visit coastal sites around Thanet, or the Observatories, when conditions are suited for falls of Scandinavian migrants – a northeasterly air flow is a vital component.

Green Woodpecker

Picus viridis

J	F	M	A	M	J	J	A	S	O	N	D

Widespread resident.   ★★★

A bird of mature, deciduous woodland, with areas of short grass, where it can feed on ants. Parkland is ideal.
Listen for its loud, laughing call-note, from which it gets its old English name 'yaffle'.

Great Spotted Woodpecker

Dendrocopos major

J	F	M	A	M	J	J	A	S	O	N	D

Widespread resident.   ★★★

Commonly associated with mature trees, it is generally absent as a breeding species from the county's marshland areas. Occasionally, in autumn, an influx of Continental migrants may occur on the coast, but the dispersal of Kent bred birds probably accounts for most isolated sightings.
The courtship 'drumming' is often the first sign of the bird's presence.

Lesser Spotted Woodpecker   *Dendrocopos minor*

J	F	M	A	M	J	J	A	S	O	N	D

Resident.   ★★★

The least common of the three woodpeckers, but quite widespread in mature woodland. Often associated, too, with alders and birches.

The 'butterfly' display flight is a delightful spectacle, but not often seen. Again, the drumming in spring and the distinctive call-note are the best guides to its presence.

Crested Lark   *Galerida cristata*

Very rare vagrant.

One at Dungeness in autumn 1975 is only the second county record and the first this century.

Woodlark   *Lullula arborea*

J	F	M	A	M	J	J	A	S	O	N	D

Passage migrant.

On average, just six records occur annually, totalling 8–10 birds. Most often seen in autumn at regularly watched coastal sites, like Thanet, St. Margaret's, or Dungeness.

Skylark   *Alauda arvensis*

J	F	M	A	M	J	J	A	S	O	N	D

Abundant resident, passage migrant and winter visitor.   ★★★

Huge diurnal movements may be witnessed at coastal sites, particularly during October, while severe weather conditions may cause cold weather movements. Quite large flocks may form in the winter months.

Sings from the ground as well as in the air, but beware, it is a good mimic of wader calls. Variations in plumage and structure, according to the prevailing conditions, can make this species a source of confusion – long-legged like a pipit or short-tailed like a Woodlark.

Shore Lark   *Eremophila alpestris*

J	F	M	A	M	J	J	A	S	O	N	D

Annual winter visitor.

Numbers fluctuate considerably from year to year and it has been relatively scarce in very recent winters. Favours shingle shores, like those at Sandwich Bay, Reculver, or Shellness, but also feeds on short grass.

Sand Martin
Riparia riparia

J	F	M	A	M	J	J	A	S	O	N	D

Summer visitor and passage migrant. ★★★

Breeding colonies are essentially associated with sand and gravel workings along the greensand belt. In September, large roosts of several thousands may be seen in reedbed localities, like those at Murston and Stodmarsh, or in Cliffe quarries.

Swallow
Hirundo rustica

J	F	M	A	M	J	J	A	S	O	N	D

Widespread summer visitor and passage migrant. ★★★

In autumn, large diurnal movements may be seen, particularly around the coast, involving day-totals of several thousand birds. Reedbed roosts may also involve similar numbers.

Red-rumped Swallow
Hirundo daurica

Very rare vagrant.

One was seen at Bough Beech in August 1972, while three May records include singles at Stodmarsh in 1973 and 1975, and at Dungeness in 1976.

House Martin
Delichon urbica

J	F	M	A	M	J	J	A	S	O	N	D

Widespread summer visitor and passage migrant. ★★★

Large, diurnal, autumn movements may involve up to 8,000 birds in a day.
  The gathering of the autumn flocks over water, on telegraph wires, or warm roof tops can be a fascinating spectacle.

Richard's Pipit
Anthus novaeseelandiae

J	F	M	A	M	J	J	A	S	O	N	D

Rare passage migrant.

Ten of the thirteen records have been reported from Sandwich Bay or Thanet.
  Richard's and young Tawny Pipits do provide identification problems. Try to describe the calls as fully as possible and note as much plumage detail as you can. The former is browner and more heavily streaked – like a Skylark.

Tawny Pipit
Anthus campestris

J F M A M J J A S O N D

Scarce passage migrant.

Almost annual, with a peak of nine records in 1971. Around the coast there have been 16 records at Dungeness, four at St. Margaret's, eight at Sandwich Bay, five on Thanet, three at Reculver and two at Shellness, with just two inland.

Beware possible confusion between young, female Yellow Wagtails and adult Tawny Pipits.

Tree Pipit
Anthus trivialis

J F M A M J J A S O N D

Summer visitor and passage migrant. ★★★

Fairly widespread, favouring coppiced areas, which provide suitable open areas for breeding and scattered solitary trees as song posts.

The 'parachuting' display flight, typical of all pipits, is a delight to watch.

Meadow Pipit
Anthus pratensis

J F M A M J J A S O N D

Resident and passage migrant. ★★★

Quite widespread in suitably damp habitats during the winter months, but favours coastal marshlands during the breeding season, though a few pairs breed at inland localities.

Red-throated Pipit
Anthus cervinus

Very rare vagrant.

One at the Sevenoaks Reserve in May 1980 is only the fourth county record.

Rock Pipit
Anthus spinoletta petrosus

J F M A M J J A S O N D

Winter visitor. ★★

Essentially a coastal species, commonly frequenting the muddy creeks and rocky shores around north and east Kent, but relatively scarce south from Folkestone.

Separating birds of the Scandinavian race *A.s.littoralis* is a challenge for your field craft and probably only possible in spring.

119

Water Pipit
A.s.spinoletta

J	F	M	A	M	J	J	A	S	O	N	D

Winter visitor and passage migrant.

A few winter fairly regularly in the Stour Valley, with small numbers roosting at Stodmarsh.
An attractive bird in breeding plumage, worth looking for in April around reservoirs, gravel pits and cress beds.

Yellow Wagtail
Motacilla flava flavissima

J	F	M	A	M	J	J	A	S	O	N	D

Summer visitor.   ***

Commonly seen on the coastal lowlands, but a few pairs breed at inland localities, along rivers, or at gravel pits. More widespread on autumn passage, when roosts of up to 300 birds may be found in reedbeds.
A number of different races can be separated in the field and the **Blue-headed Wagtail** *M.f.flava* occurs annually on spring migration and has bred. Birds showing the characteristics of the **Grey-headed Wagtail** *M.f.thunbergi* and the **Ashy-headed Wagtail** *M.f.cinereocapilla* have been recorded; however, hybridisation does occur and many variants result – a complex, but fascinating subject for some.

Grey Wagtail
Motacilla cinerea

J	F	M	A	M	J	J	A	S	O	N	D

Resident.   ***

Prefers fast flowing waterways, but is attracted to weirs and waterfalls on slower streams, which form the tributaries of the three main river systems in the county. Occurs at Dungeness on autumn passage, while in winter it can be expected in more widespread localities, including sewage farms and gravel pits.
A most attractive wagtail. Get to know its distinctive call to locate it more easily.

Pied Wagtail
Motacilla alba yarrelii

J	F	M	A	M	J	J	A	S	O	N	D

Widespread resident.   ***

Frequently forms roosts of up to 200 birds, usually in reedbeds, but sometimes in warmer zones created by man, such as in glasshouses or industrial estates.
The Continental race, the **White Wagtail** *M.a.alba* occurs regularly in spring, but is more difficult to identify in the autumn.

Waxwing
Bombycilla garrulus

J	F	M	A	M	J	J	A	S	O	N	D

Occasional winter visitor.

Ones and twos are seen almost annually, but the last irruption of this species in Kent was in 1970/71, when over 200 were present during December.

Cotoneaster berries are a favourite food when they do come and another irruption is long overdue!

Dipper
Cinclus cinclus

Very rare vagrant.

Just five birds have been seen, two of them wintering along the Loose and Len Valleys in Maidstone, the others at Sandwich Bay, Sandling Park and Otford. The extreme dates are 31st October – 12th March.

Wren
Troglodytes troglodytes

J	F	M	A	M	J	J	A	S	O	N	D

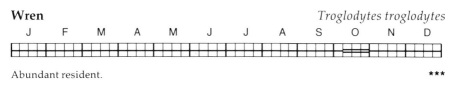

Abundant resident. ★★★

A small autumn passage is recorded at the Observatories and other regularly watched coastal sites.

Dunnock
Prunella modularis

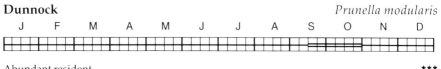

| J | F | M | A | M | J | J | A | S | O | N | D |

Abundant resident. ★★★

A small spring and autumn passage is recorded at the Observatories and other regularly watched coastal sites.

Take a close look at the attractive plumages of this and the previous species – all too often ignored, because they are so common.

Alpine Accentor
Prunella collaris

Very rare vagrant.

Remarkably, the second and third county records of this species concerned singles seen, within a day of each other, in May 1975 and 1976.

Robin
Erithacus rubecula

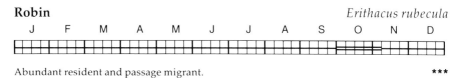

| J | F | M | A | M | J | J | A | S | O | N | D |

Abundant resident and passage migrant. ★★★

In certain weather conditions in autumn marked falls of this species may be evident around the coast, involving migrants from Scandinavia.

Nightingale
Luscinia megarhynchos

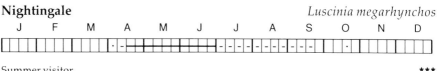

| J | F | M | A | M | J | J | A | S | O | N | D |

Summer visitor. ★★★

Most common in the south and east, with small pockets of breeding populations elsewhere. Shows a preference for woods with dense understories of hazel, hornbeam and hawthorn. When not singing they are difficult birds to locate, hence the paucity of autumn records.

Bluethroat
Luscinia svecica

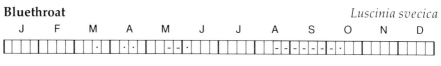

| J | F | M | A | M | J | J | A | S | O | N | D |

Scarce passage migrant.

A skulking species that is easily overlooked, inevitably most often recorded at the two Observatories.

Black Redstart
Phoenicurus ochruros

J F M A M J J A S O N D

Local breeding species, winter visitor and passage migrant. ***

A predominantly coastal species in Kent, though it may be seen in widespread localities on migration.

Visit Dungeness during migration peaks, preferably in spring, to see the attractive cock bird in breeding plumage.

Redstart
Phoenicurus phoenicurus

J F M A M J J A S O N D

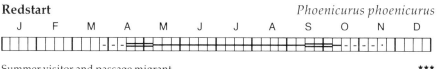

Summer visitor and passage migrant. ***

Thinly distributed as a breeding species, possibly on the decline still. Passage may be quite marked around the coast, particularly at Dungeness. In autumn, migrants can be expected in widespread inland localities too.

Redstarts require old timber for breeding, and prefer open, mixed woodland. Try Knole Park in May–June, when the cock birds are still in good plumage.

Whinchat
Saxicola rubetra

J F M A M J J A S O N D

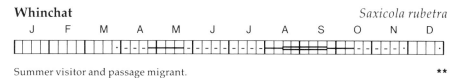

Summer visitor and passage migrant. **

Occasionally breeds on the coastal marshlands. Autumn passage may be quite marked, with falls around the coast and regular sightings at inland localities.

Stonechat
Saxicola torquata

J F M A M J J A S O N D

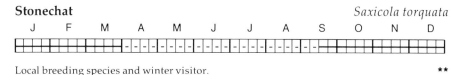

Local breeding species and winter visitor. **

A few pairs breed in most years around the coast. A marked influx is often observed in October, when numbers build up around the coast and, in recent years, a few have wintered at inland sites.

Wheatear   *Oenanthe oenanthe*

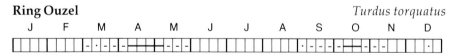

Summer visitor and passage migrant.   ★★★

Breeds regularly at Dungeness, but rarely elsewhere in the county. On migration, may be expected in widespread localities, with large falls around the coast in autumn and occasionally in spring.

Look for larger birds of the Greenland race *O.o.leucorrha* later in May, particularly at Dungeness.

Black-eared Wheatear   *Oenanthe hispanica*

Very rare vagrant.

The only county record concerns two present on Dengemarsh in May 1974.

Rock Thrush   *Monticola saxatilis*

Very rare vagrant.

The second county record concerns one present at Minster, Sheppey in February–March 1983.

Swainson's Thrush   *Catharus ustulatus*

Very rare vagrant.

The only county record of this North American species concerns one trapped at Sandwich Bay in October 1976.

Ring Ouzel   *Turdus torquatus*

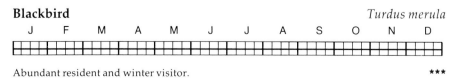

Annual passage migrant.

Occasionally seen in quite widespread localities across the county, but most often recorded at regularly watched coastal sites, like Dungeness. The largest numbers usually occur in October, though there was a heavy spring fall in May 1980.

Blackbird   *Turdus merula*

Abundant resident and winter visitor.   ★★★

Winter numbers are increased by the arrival of Continental migrants during October–November and the largest roosts may contain up to several thousand birds.

Fieldfare
Turdus pilaris

J	F	M	A	M	J	J	A	S	O	N	D

Widespread winter visitor and passage migrant.

The main arrival normally takes place in October, but large movements may also be witnessed in November. Numbers increase again on return passage during March and early April. Daily roost movements may be a feature of the winter months.

Song Thrush
Turdus philomelos

J	F	M	A	M	J	J	A	S	O	N	D

Abundant resident and winter visitor. ★★★

Winter numbers are increased with the arrival of Continental migrants during October–November.

Redwing
Turdus iliacus

J	F	M	A	M	J	J	A	S	O	N	D

Widespread winter visitor and passage migrant. ★★

A few pairs now breed almost annually. Large diurnal movements may be witnessed in October–November, but listen too for the long 'tseeep' call-note from the nocturnal migrants. Numbers increase again on return migration in March.
    Listen for the most attractive, fluty, descending notes of the spring song.

Mistle Thrush
Turdus viscivorus

J	F	M	A	M	J	J	A	S	O	N	D

Abundant resident. ★★★

In the summer months, family parties may form post-breeding flocks of 30 or more.
    Beware – the highly speckled young may cause confusion with other, less common species.

Cetti's Warbler
Cettia cetti

J	F	M	A	M	J	J	A	S	O	N	D

Locally common resident. ★★

A recent colonist now breeding annually, but spreading very slowly from its stronghold in the Stour Valley.
    Listen for its explosive, unmistakeable song from any wet habitat.

Grasshopper Warbler
Locustella naevia

J	F	M	A	M	J	J	A	S	O	N	D

Summer visitor. ★★★

Probably declining as a breeding species, with a very thin, localised distribution across the county. A skulking species, invariably located only by its reeling song, hence the paucity of autumn records.

Savi's Warbler
Locustella luscinioides

J	F	M	A	M	J	J	A	S	O	N	D

Very local summer visitor. ★★

A few pairs breed most years in the Stour Valley.

Listen for the reeling song from the reedbeds or sallows, but beware confusion with the very similar, though higher pitched, more mechanical and often more prolonged reeling of the Grasshopper Warbler.

Aquatic Warbler
Acrocephalus paludicola

J	F	M	A	M	J	J	A	S	O	N	D

Very rare vagrant.

Only ten records, five at the Observatories, three at Cliffe and one each on Thanet and Elmley.

Take care not to be confused by the yellowish-buff plumage of young Sedge Warblers.

Sedge Warbler
Acrocephalus schoenobaenus

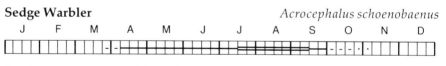

J	F	M	A	M	J	J	A	S	O	N	D

Locally numerous summer visitor and passage migrant. ★★★

Breeds commonly on the coastal marshlands and in the Stour Valley reedbeds, with smaller numbers at other, suitable inland localities. More widespread on autumn passage.

Marsh Warbler
Acrocephalus palustris

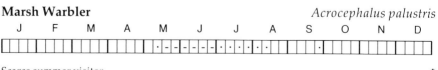

J	F	M	A	M	J	J	A	S	O	N	D

Scarce summer visitor. ★

Increasingly recorded on spring migration and probably breeding more regularly than we are aware. Most easily located by its mimetic song.

A difficult species to identify with certainty, unless it is singing well. However, the clean 'tuc' call-note certainly separates it from the Reed Warbler.

Reed Warbler   *Acrocephalus scirpaceus*

J	F	M	A	M	J	J	A	S	O	N	D

Locally numerous summer visitor and passage migrant.   ★★★

Wherever *phragmites* reedbeds occur, this species can be expected. Where a large population exists, it may move into nearby, drier vegetation to breed. On migration it occurs in a wide variety of habitats, when it may cause problems of identification.

This species is also capable of mimetic song, so check most carefully.

Great Reed Warbler   *Acrocephalus arundinaceus*

J	F	M	A	M	J	J	A	S	O	N	D

Very rare vagrant.

Seven in the Stour Valley, two at Dungeness and one on Elmley, with only three since 1974, summarises the current situation.

Icterine Warbler   *Hippolais icterina*

J	F	M	A	M	J	J	A	S	O	N	D

Annual passage migrant.

The majority of records come from the two Observatories, but other regularly watched coastal sites, in particular Thanet, are now producing increasingly more frequent sightings.

This and the next species can be difficult to separate. Try to note wing length, head shape and leg colour accurately, as well as full plumage details. It is by a combination of several characteristics, rather than any one, that satisfactory conclusions may be drawn.

Melodious Warbler   *Hippolais polyglotta*

J	F	M	A	M	J	J	A	S	O	N	D

Rare passage migrant.

Most records come from the two Observatories again.

Take care over possible confusion with brightly plumaged immature Willow Warblers in autumn.

Dartford Warbler
Sylvia undata

J	F	M	A	M	J	J	A	S	O	N	D

Rare vagrant.

Just thirteen records, of single birds, all but two from Dungeness.

Subalpine Warbler
Sylvia cantillans

Very rare vagrant.

Singles at Dungeness in October 1976 and at Sandwich Bay and Dungeness again in June 1979 are the only county records.

Sardinian Warbler
Sylvia melanocephala

Very rare vagrant.

The only county record concerns one at Dungeness in April 1973.

Barred Warbler
Sylvia nisoria

J	F	M	A	M	J	J	A	S	O	N	D

Rare passage migrant.

Thanet has produced seven records of this skulking species in recent years, all but one of the other thirteen, a freshly dead bird found at Kennington in November 1971, have been at the two Observatories.

Lesser Whitethroat
Sylvia curruca

J	F	M	A	M	J	J	A	S	O	N	D

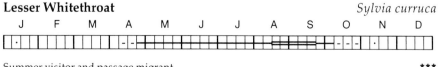

Summer visitor and passage migrant.   ★★★

Falls of migrants may be witnessed, more often in autumn, at the Observatories or other regularly watched coastal sites. Most easily located in spring by its song – a rattle-like repetition of a single note, which may be preceded, or followed by a musical warbling.

Whitethroat *Sylvia communis*

J	F	M	A	M	J	J	A	S	O	N	D

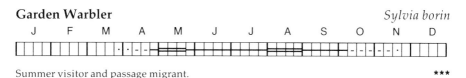

Summer visitor and passage migrant. ★★★

Though the population is probably smaller than it was in the sixties – prior to the collapse in 1969 attributed to the prolonged drought in the southern Sahel (Winstanley, D. *et al.* 1974)* – the Whitethroat is still well distributed throughout the county as a breeding species. Falls of migrants are reported from regularly watched coastal sites, more often in autumn than in spring, though the largest involved 200 at Dungeness in May 1980.

*see Where have all the Whitethroats gone? *Bird Study* 21:1–14.

Garden Warbler *Sylvia borin*

J	F	M	A	M	J	J	A	S	O	N	D

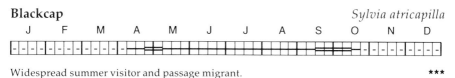

Summer visitor and passage migrant. ★★★

Widespread, but slightly less common than the next species, favouring similar, deciduous woodland habitat.

One of the most non-descript species I know, most easily located, in spring, by its song, an attractive, full-toned, fairly uniformly pitched warble.

Blackcap *Sylvia atricapilla*

J	F	M	A	M	J	J	A	S	O	N	D

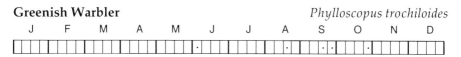

Widespread summer visitor and passage migrant. ★★★

A few overwinter in most years and may occasionally be seen feeding at bird tables.

The song is much more varied in pitch than that of the previous species, though the sub-song is very similar.

Greenish Warbler *Phylloscopus trochiloides*

J	F	M	A	M	J	J	A	S	O	N	D

Very rare vagrant.

Just five records of single birds, three at Dungeness and one each at St. Margaret's and Sandwich Bay.

Pallas's Warbler
Phylloscopus proregulus

J	F	M	A	M	J	J	A	S	O	N	D

Rare vagrant.

Becoming annual since 1975, with four in that year and in 1982, and eight in 1980. All but four have occurred at the two Observatories.

Yellow-browed Warbler
Phylloscopus inornatus

J	F	M	A	M	J	J	A	S	O	N	D

Scarce vagrant.

Almost annual, with 22 records along the coast between Thanet, Sandwich Bay and St. Margaret's, seven at Dungeness and just four elsewhere.

Dusky Warbler
Phylloscopus fuscatus

J	F	M	A	M	J	J	A	S	O	N	D

Very rare vagrant.

Just three singles, on the Isle of Grain, at Sandwich Bay and at Dungeness. There is only one earlier Kent record.

Bonelli's Warbler
Phylloscopus bonelli

J	F	M	A	M	J	J	A	S	O	N	D

Very rare vagrant.

Just four records, three at Dungeness and one at St. Nicholas-at-Wade.

Wood Warbler
Phylloscopus sibilatrix

J	F	M	A	M	J	J	A	S	O	N	D

Summer visitor and passage migrant.   **★★**

Sadly, this attractive warbler, with its most beautiful trilling song, seems to be on the decline as a breeding species in Kent. Mature, deciduous woods, with open glades are favoured.
   Try Hungershall Park in Tunbridge Wells.

Chiffchaff

Phylloscopus collybita

J F M A M J J A S O N D

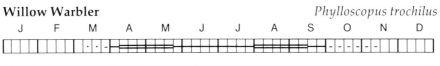

Widespread summer visitor and passage migrant. ★★★

A few overwinter in most years. Falls of migrants, most noticeable at coastal sites, are larger and more frequent in the autumn.

Most easily separated from the following species by its distinctive, onomatopoeic song. There are also subtle differences in call, plumage and wing structure, that require critical field observation. Beware the different plumages – browner above and whiter below – of the northern and eastern races that also occur in Kent in late autumn.

Willow Warbler

Phylloscopus trochilus

J F M A M J J A S O N D

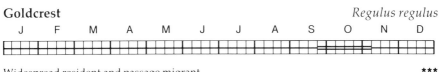

Abundant summer visitor and passage migrant. ★★★

Marked falls of migrants may occur at coastal localities in both spring and autumn, while sudden increases inland may also be noticeable.

There is a northern race of this species too, which may cause confusion at times.

Goldcrest

Regulus regulus

J F M A M J J A S O N D

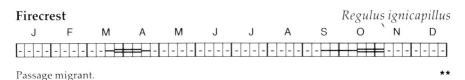

Widespread resident and passage migrant. ★★★

Autumn passage may involve marked falls of several hundred birds, most obvious at coastal localities like Dungeness, where the relatively sparse vegetation can come alive with these tiny migrants.

Firecrest

Regulus ignicapillus

J F M A M J J A S O N D

Passage migrant. ★★

Seemingly on the increase, a few now winter, most regularly at Dungeness, and small breeding populations have been discovered in recent years.

This tiny, most attractively plumaged bird, can be seen quite easily at Dungeness when on passage, while its subtly different call and song may be heard, particularly in mature plantations of Norway spruce, in late spring and summer.

131

Spotted Flycatcher

Muscicapa striata

J	F	M	A	M	J	J	A	S	O	N	D

Widespread summer visitor and passage migrant.   ★★★

The largest falls of migrants have occurred in spring. Look for the delightfully 'spotted' young in July and August.

Red-breasted Flycatcher

Ficedula parva

J	F	M	A	M	J	J	A	S	O	N	D

Scarce passage migrant.

One to four are recorded annually, most often along the coast between Thanet and St. Margaret's.

Another delightful little bird, but it can be very difficult to see when feeding in the high canopy. Sadly, the orange-breasted male is very rarely seen in Kent.

Pied Flycatcher

Ficedula hypoleuca

J	F	M	A	M	J	J	A	S	O	N	D

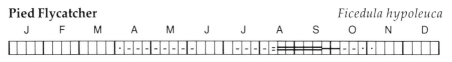

Passage migrant.

Comparatively few are seen on spring passage, but in autumn, they may appear in widespread localities, with falls of 30 or more at the Observatories and other regularly watched coastal sites.

Bearded Tit
Panurus biarmicus

J F M A M J J A S O N D

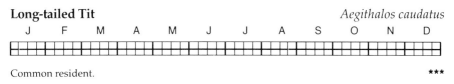

Local resident and passage migrant.   ★★★

Stodmarsh holds a large breeding population, but small colonies exist elsewhere in *phragmites* reedbeds. In autumn our own birds disperse and the numbers are increased by the arrival of migrants, which may turn up in widespread localities, some remaining to winter.
  Visit Stodmarsh in September to witness their irruptive behaviour.

Long-tailed Tit
Aegithalos caudatus

J F M A M J J A S O N D

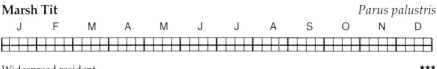

Common resident.   ★★★

A most attractive species, forming loose flocks in the winter months.

Marsh Tit
Parus palustris

J F M A M J J A S O N D

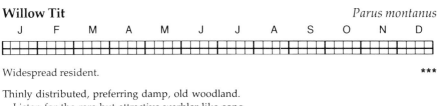

Widespread resident.   ★★★

Commonly found along the wooded downland.
  The two black-headed tits are quite difficult to separate at times, but there are subtle differences in their structure and plumage. Get to know their calls. The 'pitchu' call-note of the Marsh Tit is quite diagnostic – but beware the imitative Great Tit!

Willow Tit
Parus montanus

J F M A M J J A S O N D

Widespread resident.   ★★★

Thinly distributed, preferring damp, old woodland.
  Listen for the rare but attractive warbler like song.

Coal Tit
Parus ater

J F M A M J J A S O N D

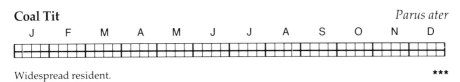

Widespread resident.   ★★★

This species shows a marked preference for conifers. Continental birds, with whiter head markings and greyer mantles, may be seen along the east coast in autumn.

Blue Tit

Parus caeruleus

J	F	M	A	M	J	J	A	S	O	N	D

Common resident. ★★★

Autumn flocks may be increased with the arrival of migrants from the Continent and small falls may be witnessed around the coast.

Great Tit

Parus major

J	F	M	A	M	J	J	A	S	O	N	D

Common resident. ★★★

Small groups of Continental migrants may be seen around the coast in autumn.
  Be aware of this species' ability to mimic the calls of other passerines.

Nuthatch

Sitta europaea

J	F	M	A	M	J	J	A	S	O	N	D

Locally common resident. ★★★

Favours suitably mature, deciduous woodland and parkland. Most easily located by its distinctive calls and song, particularly the far-carrying 'tiu-tiu-tiu'.

Treecreeper

Certhia familiaris

J	F	M	A	M	J	J	A	S	O	N	D

Widespread resident. ★★★

Familiarity with the thin call-note and attractive, high-pitched song is important in locating this inconspicuous, mouse-like bird.

Short-toed Treecreeper

Certhia brachydactyla

Very rare vagrant.

Singles at Worth in September 1973 and Sandwich Bay in April 1974, two at Dungeness in October 1978 and another at St. Margaret's in September 1983 were all trapped and ringed. There is only one previous county record.

  An extremely difficult species to identify with certainty in the field, but characteristically duller, with off-white underparts.

Penduline Tit
Remiz pendulinus

Very rare vagrant.

The first county record concerns one at Stodmarsh in May 1980, followed by another there and two migrants at St. Margaret's in autumn 1983.
Could this species be the next to colonise Kent?

Golden Oriole
Oriolus oriolus

J	F	M	A	M	J	J	A	S	O	N	D

Annual visitor in very small numbers. ★★

The majority of sightings may be expected in east Kent, where breeding has been proved in recent years, or at coastal sites, like Dungeness, during spring migration.
Despite the brilliant yellow plumage, they become almost invisible in leafy foliage. Get to know the distinctive calls.

Red-backed Shrike
Lanius collurio

J	F	M	A	M	J	J	A	S	O	N	D

Passage migrant. ★★

Virtually lost as a breeding species, but a few are seen annually, most frequently around the coast on autumn passage.

Lesser Grey Shrike
Lanius minor

Very rare vagrant.

Only three records, all of singles, near Wye in September 1976, at Seasalter in June 1977 and at nearby Chislet in June 1980. There are just two earlier county records.

Great Grey Shrike
Lanius excubitor

J	F	M	A	M	J	J	A	S	O	N	D

Winter visitor and passage migrant.

Autumn migrants may be expected around the east coast. Wintering birds may turn up in widespread localities, often returning to the same site year after year, though their winter territories may be quite large.
Stodmarsh is the most regularly visited winter haunt.

Woodchat Shrike
Lanius senator

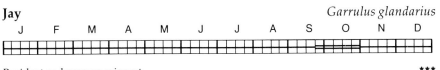

Rare passage migrant.

All but two have occurred along the coast between Thanet and Dungeness, where six individuals have been seen.

Jay
Garrulus glandarius

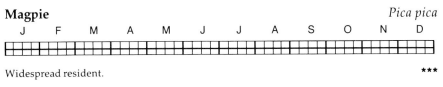

Resident and passage migrant. ***

In autumn, small numbers may be seen on passage, with occasional irruptive movements from the Continent.

Magpie
Pica pica

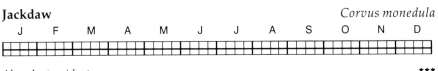

Widespread resident. ***

May be seen in sizeable flocks in the winter months.

Nutcracker
Nucifraga caryocatactes

Very rare vagrant.

Two were seen at Bedgebury in December 1972.

Jackdaw
Corvus monedula

Abundant resident. ***

Flocks of several hundred form during the winter months and may be seen flying to and from their roosts. Westerly movements in the autumn may involve Continental birds.

Rook

Corvus frugilegus

J F M A M J J A S O N D

Widespread resident.   ★★★

Large flocks gather for feeding and roosting. A few rookeries too may contain as many as 100–300 pairs. Westerly movements in the autumn may involve Continental birds.

Carrion Crow

Corvus corone corone

J F M A M J J A S O N D

Widespread resident.   ★★★

Although generally more solitary than the Rook, flocks of up to 200 may gather to feed, particularly at rubbish tips.

Hooded Crow

C.c.cornix

J F M A M J J A S O N D

Annual winter visitor and passage migrant.

Becoming relatively scarce. Most frequently seen on the coastal marshlands, but may be attracted to rubbish tips throughout the county.

Raven

Corvus corax

J F M A M J J A S O N D

Possible vagrant.

The occasional, mainly inland sightings, may refer to escaped birds.

Starling

Sturnus vulgaris

J F M A M J J A S O N D

Abundant resident, passage migrant and winter visitor.   ★★★

In autumn, impressive numbers of Continental birds may be seen moving in a westerly direction, while winter roosts, which may contain up to a million birds, can also provide quite spectacular sights.

Rose-coloured Starling
Sturnus roseus

Very rare vagrant.

Singles occurred at Sandwich in September and Canterbury in November 1971, at Sandwich again in February 1972 and Northward Hill in May 1976.

House Sparrow
Passer domesticus

| J | F | M | A | M | J | J | A | S | O | N | D |

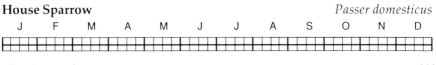

Abundant resident.   ★★★

An adaptable, opportunist feeder and large numbers may be seen, particularly amongst cereal crops, both before and after harvest. Roosts in dense hedgerows may also involve several thousand birds.

Tree Sparrow
Passer montanus

| J | F | M | A | M | J | J | A | S | O | N | D |

Widespread resident.   ★★★

Small flocks of several hundred birds may build up in autumn, remain together during the winter months, wherever food is readily available, and increase again in spring, before dispersing to breed. Some diurnal passage can also be witnessed around the coast in spring and autumn.

A smart little sparrow, with a noticeable white collar.

Chaffinch
Fringilla coelebs

| J | F | M | A | M | J | J | A | S | O | N | D |

Widespread resident, passage migrant and winter visitor.   ★★★

Winter flocks may be increased by the arrival of Continental migrants and diurnal passage can be particularly well marked during the autumn.

Brambling
Fringilla montifringilla

| J | F | M | A | M | J | J | A | S | O | N | D |

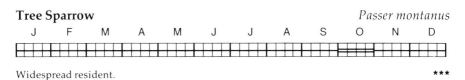

Winter visitor and passage migrant.

The numbers vary considerably from year to year. Although beech mast is one of the favoured foods, Bramblings may frequently join mixed finch flocks in a variety of agricultural habitats.

Get to know the distinctive call-notes to locate them amongst migrant Chaffinch flocks, or flying to roost – at Bedgebury for example.

Serin
Serinus serinus

J	F	M	A	M	J	J	A	S	O	N	D

Scarce passage migrant.

The majority of records have occurred at Dungeness, but it is being recorded with increasing regularity in Thanet.

It is essential to know the distinctive call-notes in order to locate this species, as it often just flies overhead.

Greenfinch
Carduelis chloris

J	F	M	A	M	J	J	A	S	O	N	D

Widespread resident. ★★★

The availability of food determines the size and distribution of winter flocks, which may occasionally number several thousand birds and include migrants from further north and the Continent.

Goldfinch
Carduelis carduelis

J	F	M	A	M	J	J	A	S	O	N	D

Widespread resident and passage migrant. ★★★

Flocks feeding on thistles are a typical autumn feature. At coastal localities, like Dungeness, day-totals on autumn passage may occasionally involve several thousand birds, while in severe winters very few may remain. Those that do may often be found feeding in alders.

Siskin
Carduelis spinus

J	F	M	A	M	J	J	A	S	O	N	D

Winter visitor.

Autumn migrants may be seen around the coast, or heard passing overhead, provided that you know the distinctive call-note. Flocks of 100 or more may occur in good winters, but the numbers vary considerably from year to year.

Check any damp habitat with alders, but they can be attracted to feeders, by displaying peanuts in red plastic bags!

Linnet
Carduelis cannabina

J	F	M	A	M	J	J	A	S	O	N	D

Widespread resident and passage migrant. ★★★

Post breeding flocks of a few hundred birds may frequently be seen feeding on grass seeds, while winter flocks of similar size may be found in a few coastal localities, with generally smaller numbers inland. In some winters Linnets may be quite scarce.

Twite
Carduelis flavirostris

J	F	M	A	M	J	J	A	S	O	N	D

Winter visitor.

In the early seventies flocks of up to 500 were present, but flocks of 100 are scarce now. Favours the coastal marshes in north Kent and around Sandwich Bay, often feeding on the saltings with Linnets. Very rarely seen inland.

Get to know the call to locate them, then look for the yellow bill.

Redpoll
Carduelis flammea cabaret

J	F	M	A	M	J	J	A	S	O	N	D

Resident and passage migrant. ★★★

Becoming increasingly widespread, the Redpoll favours silver birch or alder seed, but in winter may often be found feeding on willow herb, or with mixed finch flocks on fallen seeds.

The larger, greyer **Mealy Redpoll** *C.f.flammea* can occasionally be separated, usually during spring or autumn passage, but beware, as there is considerable variation in the plumages of both races.

Arctic Redpoll
Carduelis hornemanni

Very rare vagrant.

The first Kent records were of singles seen at Dungeness and Egypt Bay in October 1972, followed by others at Sevenoaks in April 1978 and Foreness Point in December 1979.

Crossbill
Loxia curvirostra

J	F	M	A	M	J	J	A	S	O	N	D

An irruptive species, almost annual. ★★

In a typical invasion year, as in 1979/80, numbers build up from July onwards, with a few remaining to breed the following summer. At other times it is relatively rare, but check conifer plantations and listen for their distinctive 'chip-chip-chip' call-notes.

Scarlet Rosefinch   *Carpodacus erythrinus*

Very rare vagrant.

One was trapped and ringed at Broadstairs in May 1971, a pair was trapped at Dungeness in June 1977 and another seen there in September 1981.

Pine Grosbeak   *Pinicola enucleator*

Very rare vagrant.

One seen near Maidstone in May 1971 is only the third Kent record.

Bullfinch   *Pyrrhula pyrrhula*

J	F	M	A	M	J	J	A	S	O	N	D

Widespread resident.   ★★★

Small flocks may be seen in the winter months, while there is some evidence of a small autumn passage in recent years.

Hawfinch   *Coccothraustes coccothraustes*

J	F	M	A	M	J	J	A	S	O	N	D

Resident.   ★★★

A very local species, but once you have got to know the distinctive calls and found a frequented locality, they can be a source of great pleasure. They form regular winter roosts, the best known of which is probably the one in Bedgebury Pinetum, which attracts 50–100 birds each winter, while Maidstone Cemetery is used regularly by a few birds. They favour the cypress trees which offer the greatest shelter.

Lapland Bunting
Calcarius lapponicus

J	F	M	A	M	J	J	A	S	O	N	D

Winter visitor and passage migrant.

The numbers vary considerably from year to year, but occasionally small flocks overwinter, favouring the coastal marshes.

The distinctive call-note is almost essential to locate them, as they are not easy to see when they disappear into long grass or stubble.

Snow Bunting
Plectrophenax nivalis

J	F	M	A	M	J	J	A	S	O	N	D

Winter visitor.

This species favours the shingle beaches along the Thames and Swale, round to Sandwich Bay. Numbers vary considerably, the largest flock, usually at Sandwich Bay, involving 100 or more birds.

Yellowhammer
Emberiza citrinella

J	F	M	A	M	J	J	A	S	O	N	D

Widespread resident. ★★★

Like other seed-eaters, this species also gathers in flocks in the winter months. At other times its song from the hedgerows is a typical sound of the countryside.

Cirl Bunting
Emberiza cirlus

J	F	M	A	M	J	J	A	S	O	N	D

Very rare vagrant.

The seven records all concern singles, apart from one flock of five, and they have been reported from widespread localities.

Ortolan Bunting   *Emberiza hortulana*

J			F			M			A			M			J			J			A			S			O			N			D		

Rare passage migrant.

All fifteen records have been around the coast, with ten at Dungeness.

Rustic Bunting   *Emberiza rustica*

Very rare vagrant.

The second and third county records concern singles in 1983 at Northward Hill in June and Dungeness in October.

Reed Bunting   *Emberiza schoeniclus*

J			F			M			A			M			J			J			A			S			O			N			D		

Abundant breeding species and passage migrant.   ★★★

Widespread in suitably damp, waterside localities, though spreading into drier habitats to breed in recent years. In winter, small numbers may join mixed finch flocks to feed on available seeds, while roosts in reedbeds may also be discovered.

Black-headed Bunting   *Emberiza melanocephala*

Very rare vagrant.

The only county records concern singles at Sandwich Bay in June 1972, Reculver in August 1973 and Dungeness in May 1983.

Corn Bunting   *Miliaria calandra*

J			F			M			A			M			J			J			A			S			O			N			D		

Resident.   ★★★

Widespread on the coastal marshes and thinly distributed along the Downs, but virtually absent from the Weald. In winter, small roosts may be established in reedbeds.

Appendix I

Species included in the Kent list, but not recorded during 1970–83.

White-billed Diver
Great Shearwater
Black Duck
King Eider
White-tailed Eagle
Golden Eagle
Lesser Kestrel
Baillon's Crake
Little Bustard
Cream-coloured Courser
Black-winged Pratincole
Laughing Gull
Ivory Gull
Bridled Tern

Pallas's Sandgrouse
Snowy Owl
Tengmalm's Owl
Rufous Bush Robin
Thrush Nightingale
Red-flanked Bluetail
Black Wheatear
Moustached Warbler
Olivaceous Warbler
Radde's Warbler
Chough
Slate-coloured Junco
Rock Bunting
Little Bunting

Appendix II

Gazetteer of all the place names mentioned in the text.

Ordnance Survey maps are essential to enable you to locate the place names and to follow the suggestions in the Birdwatching Calendar chapter.

Where a large area is referred to the four-figure map reference, which pin-points a 1-kilometre square, is usually towards the centre of that area where the name is printed on the 1:50,000 map. Sometimes the reference shows the square in which the site referred to lies, rather than the nearby village of that name.

The first two figures of the grid reference show the west edge of the 1-kilometre square in which the locality lies – the figures on the north and south margins of the map. The second two figures show the south edge of the 1-kilometre square – the figures on the west and east margins of the map.

Allhallows	8378	Cooling Marshes	7677
Aylesford	7258	Copperhouse Marshes	8069
		Copt Point	2436
Barksore	8768		
Bartlett Creek	8269	Deal	3752
Bedgebury Pinetum	7233	Dengemarsh	0518
Bewl Bridge N.R.	6731	Detling	7958
Bewl Bridge Reservoir	6733	Dover	3241
Birchington	3069	Dungeness Bird Observatory	0817
Blean Wood	0860	Dungeness RSPB Reserve	0618
Bough Beech Reservoir	4948		
Boughton Monchelsea	7749	East Sutton	8348
Boughton Park	7749	Eastwell Park	0146
Broadstairs	3967	Egypt Bay	7779
Broomfield	8452	Elmley RSPB Reserve	9567
Burham Marsh	7161		
		Fagg's Wood	9834
Canterbury	1457	Fairfield	9626
Capel Fleet	0068	Folkestone Harbour	2335
Capel Hill	0069	Folkestone Warren	2437
Challock Forest	0350	Fordwich	1859
Chartham	1055	Foreness Point	3871
Chilham	0653	Funton Creek	8868
Chislet Marsh	2366		
Chetney Marshes	8871	Grain	8976
Church Wood	1059	Graveney Marshes	0664
Cliffe Pools	7277	Gravesend	6474
Cliffe Quarry	7275	Greatstone	0823
		Grove Ferry	2362

Half Acre	8369	Otford	5259
Ham Green	8469	Park Wood, Maidstone	7852
Hamstreet Wood	0033	Pegwell Bay	3563
Harrietsham	8753	Port Regis	3970
Harty, Ferry House Inn	0165		
Haysden	5645	Rainham Creek	8268
Headcorn	8344	Reculver	2269
Hersden Lake	2061	Romney Marsh	0429
Hollingbourne	8455	Rough Common	1259
Hungershall Park	5738	St. Margaret's Bay	3543
Hurst Wood, Mereworth	6254	St. Nicholas-at-Wade	2766
		Sandling Park	1436
Isle of Grain Power Station	8975	Sayes Court	0266
		Sevenoaks Reserve	5256
Kingsnorth	8172	Sharp's Green	8268
Kingswood	8151	Shellness, Sheppey	0567
Knole Park	5453	Shoreham	5161
		Six Mile Cottages	1344
Lade Pits	0721	South Swale N.R.	0364
Lade Sands	0820	Sportsman Inn	0664
Langley Park Farm	7951	Stodmarsh	2160
Leeds Castle	8352	Stoke Lagoon	8576
Leybourne Lakes	6959	Stonar Lake	3359
Leysdown	0370	Stonelees	3462
Loose	7652	Sutton Valence	8149
Lower Halstow	8667	Swanscombe	6075
Luddesdown	6766	Swigshole Cottage	7877
Lyminge Forest	1343		
		Thornden Wood	1463
Manston Airport	3366	Trenley Park Wood	1959
Margate	3571	Tunbridge Wells	5839
Marshside	2266		
Minnis Bay	2769	Walland Marsh	9823
Minster, Sheppey	9573	Wantsum Marsh	2466
Mocketts	0166	Warden Point	0272
Mote Park	7755	Westbere	1960
Motney Hill	8268	Westwell	9947
Murston	9265	Whiteness	3970
		Whitstable	1066
New Hythe	7060	Windmill Creek	9668
Nor Marsh	8169	Woolpack	9724
Northdown Park	3770		
North Foreland	4069	Yantlet Creek	8578
Northward Hill	7876		

Appendix III

Addresses of Organizations and Reserves mentioned in the text.

Church Wood RSPB Reserve
Warden, 32 Hillview Road, Canterbury CT2 8EX.
Access from Rough Common along public footpaths.

Dungeness Bird Observatory
Sean McMinn, DBO, Dungeness, Romney Marsh TN29 9NA.

Dungeness RSPB Reserve
Peter Makepeace, Boulderwall Farm, Dungeness Road, Lydd TN29 9PN.
Open 1030–1700 W Sa Su, also Th Apr–Sept.

Elmley RSPB Reserve
Bob Gomes, Kingshill Farm, Elmley, Sheerness, Isle of Sheppey ME12 3RW.
Open 1000–1800 W Sa Su. Access from A249.

Kent Ornithological Society
Secretary: P.C. Heathcote, 5 Cedar Close, Meopham, Gravesend DA13 0ED.
KBR Editor: A.C.B. Henderson, Perry Fields Cottage, Wingham, Canterbury CT3 1ER.
Kent Bird Report: from R.W. George, 10 Dence Park, Herne Bay CT6 6BG.

Kent Trust for Nature Conservation
F. Booth, 125 High Street, Rainham ME8 8AN.

Northward Hill RSPB Reserve
Alan Parker, Swigshole Cottage, High Halstow, Rochester.
Access on footpaths from Northwood Avenue, High Halstow.

Royal Society for the Protection of Birds
The Lodge, Sandy, Bedfordshire SG19 2DL.

RSPB Local Members' Groups
Canterbury: John Cantelo, 17 Clyde Street, Canterbury.
Gravesend: Jim Martin, 43 Wilson Avenue, Rochester.
Maidstone: Denise Morgan, 1 Somerfield Close, Maidstone.
Medway: Alan Pease, 16 Copperhouse Road, Strood.
Sevenoaks: David Perry, Beech Hill, Pilgrim's Way, Kemsing, Sevenoaks.
South East: Clifford Percival, 4 Hylands Row, Woodchurch, Ashford.
Thanet: Brian Summerfield, Balcombe House, 11a Avenue Gardens, Margate.
Tonbridge: Toddy Last, 2 Guestwick, Tonbridge.

Sandwich Bay Bird Observatory
Ian Hunter, SBBO, Guilford Road, Sandwich Bay CT13 9PF.

Sevenoaks Wildfowl Reserve
John Tyler, Tadorna, Bradbourne Vale Road, Sevenoaks TN13 3DH.

Index to Systematic List

Meresborough Books

Proprietors Hamish and Barbara Mackay Miller
7 STATION ROAD, RAINHAM, GILLINGHAM, KENT. ME8 7RS
Telephone Medway (0634) 371591

We are a specialist publisher of books about Kent. Our books are available in most bookshops in the county, including our own at this address. Alternatively you may order direct, adding 10% for post (minimum 20p, orders over £20.00 post free). ISBN prefix 0 905270. Titles in print May 1985:

BYGONE KENT. A monthly journal on all aspects of Kent history founded October 1979. £1.20 per month. Annual Subscription £13.00. All back numbers available.

HARDBACKS

ROCHESTER FROM OLD PHOTOGRAPHS compiled by the City of Rochester Society. Large format. ISBN 975. £7.95. (Also available in paperback ISBN 983. £4.95.)

THE LONDON, CHATHAM & DOVER RAILWAY by Adrian Gray. A major study of the development of railways in Kent. ISBN 886. £7.95.

THE NATURAL HISTORY OF ROMNEY MARSH by Dr F.M. Firth, M.A., Ph.D. ISBN 789. £6.95.

O FAMOUS KENT by Eric Swain. The county of Kent in old prints. ISBN 738. £9.95. BARGAIN OFFER £4.95.

KENT'S OWN by Robin J. Brooks. The history of 500 (County of Kent) Squadron of the R.A.A.F. ISBN 541. £5.95.

TWO HALVES OF A LIFE by Doctor Kary Pole. The autobiography of a Viennese doctor who escaped from the Nazis and established a new career in Kent. ISBN 509. £5.95.

SOUTH EAST BRITAIN: ETERNAL BATTLEGROUND by Gregory Blaxland. A military history. ISBN 444. £5.95.

THE WHITE HORSE AND THE KANGAROO by Clive W. Porter. A complete record of the cricket matches between Kent and the Australian touring teams. ISBN 312. £5.50.

KENT AIRFIELDS IN THE BATTLE OF BRITAIN by The Kent Aviation Historical Research Society. A study of nine airfields. Over 100 photographs. ISBN 363. £5.95.

HAWKINGE 1912-1961 by Roy Humphreys. A study of the former RAF Station, 100 photographs. ISBN 355. £5.95.

A NEW DICTIONARY OF KENT DIALECT by Alan Major. The first major work on the subject this century. ISBN 274. £7.50.

KENT CASTLES by John Guy. The first comprehensive guide to all the castles and castle sites in Kent. ISBN 150. £7.50.

US BARGEMEN by A.S. Bennett. A new book of sailing barge life around Kent and Essex from the author of 'June of Rochester' and 'Tide Time'. ISBN 207. £6.95.

THE GILLS by Tony Conway. A history of Gillingham Football Club. 96 large format pages packed with old photographs. ISBN 266. £5.95. BARGAIN OFFER £1.95.

A VIEW OF CHRIST'S COLLEGE, BLACKHEATH by A.E.O. Crombie, B.A. ISBN 223. £6.95.

JUST OFF THE SWALE by Don Sattin. The story of the barge-building village of Conyer. ISBN 045. £5.95.

TEYNHAM MANOR AND HUNDRED (798-1935) by Elizabeth Selby MBE. ISBN 630 £5.95.

THE PLACE NAMES OF KENT by Judith Glover. A comprehensive reference work. ISBN 614. £7.50 (also available in paperback. ISBN 622. £3.95)

CHIDDINGSTONE – AN HISTORICAL EXPLORATION by Jill Newton. An enthusiastic account of this famous Tudor village. ISBN 940. £1.95.

STOUR VALLEY WALKS from Canterbury to Sandwich by Christopher Donaldson. Enjoy six days walking along the route taken by Caesar, Hengist & Horsa, St Augustine and many others. ISBN 991. £1.95.

THE GHOSTS OF KENT by Peter Underwood, President of the Ghost Club. ISBN 86X. £3.95.

CURIOUS KENT by John Vigar. A selection of the more unusual aspects of Kent history. ISBN 878. £1.95.

REAL ALE PUBS IN KENT by CAMRA in Kent. ISBN 894. £1.50.

A CHRONOLOGY OF ROCHESTER by Brenda Purle. ISBN 851. £1.50.

SITTINGBOURNE & KEMSLEY LIGHT RAILWAY STOCKBOOK AND GUIDE. ISBN 843. 95p.

A GUIDE TO HISTORIC KENT by Irene Hales. A guide to the most interesting features of every town and village, with details of each place of historic interest open to the public. ISBN 711. £1.50.

DOVER REMEMBERED by Jessie Elizabeth Vine. Personal memories from the early years of this century. ISBN 819. £3.95.

THE PLACE NAMES OF KENT – see under hardbacks.

PENINSULA ROUND (The Hoo Peninsula) by Des Worsdale. ISBN 568. £1.50.

A HISTORY OF CHATHAM GRAMMAR SCHOOL FOR GIRLS, 1907-1982 by Audrey Perkyns. ISBN 576. £1.95.

CYCLE TOURS OF KENT by John Guy. No. 1: Medway, Gravesend, Sittingbourne and Sheppey. ISBN 517. £1.50.

THE CANTERBURY AND WHITSTABLE RAILWAY 1830-1980: A PICTORIAL SURVEY. ISBN 118. 75p.

ROCHESTER'S HERITAGE TRAIL. (Published for The City of Rochester Society.) A useful guide for the visitor to most places of interest in Rochester. ISBN 169. £1.25.

WINGS OVER KENT. A selection of articles by members of the Kent Aviation Historical Research Society. ISBN 69X. £1.95.

LULLINGSTONE PARK: THE EVOLUTION OF A MEDIAEVAL DEER PARK by Susan Pittman. ISBN 703. £3.95.

LET'S EXPLORE THE RIVER DARENT by Frederick Wood. Walking from Westerham to Dartford. ISBN 770. £1.95.

SAINT ANDREW'S CHURCH, DEAL by Gregory Holyoake. ISBN 835. 95p.

BIRDS OF KENT: A Review of their Status and Distribution. A reprint, with addendum, of the 448 page study by the Kent Ornithological Society. ISBN 800. £6.95.

Further titles are in preparation. Details will be announced in 'Bygone Kent'.